LINCOLNSHIRE

Matthew Pike

COUNTRYSIDE BOOKS

NEWBURY BERKSHIRE

COUNTRYSIDE BOOKS
3 Catherine Road
Newbury, Berkshire

To view our complete range of books,
please visit us at
www.countrysidebooks.co.uk

ISBN: 978 1 84674 142 5

Maps by Gelder Design & Mapping
Photographs by the author

Designed by Peter Davies, Nautilus Design
Produced through MRM Associates Ltd., Reading
Typeset by Jean Cussons Typesetting, Diss, Norfolk
Printed in Thailand

CONTENTS

Introduction

So **many people believe that** exercise involves pumping weights, breaking pain barriers, and spending vast sums of money for the privilege. But experts say regular moderate exercise is a fantastic way to keep fit and stay healthy. A programme of frequent walks can help your body in so many ways, from improving your heart and circulation to boosting the immune system, assisting weight loss, lowering blood and cholesterol levels, strengthening and improving the flexibility of muscles and bones. On top of that, walking is free to do, sociable and great fun!

Whether you feel unfit and would like to improve your health, you want to lose weight, or you simply feel in good shape and wish to stay that way, regular walks combined with a healthy diet will help you achieve your goals.

In this book I have scanned the whole county to find attractive, enjoyable walks to help you on your way. Lincolnshire is blessed with the rolling hills of the Wolds, ancient woodland, sandy beaches, rare marshland, picture postcard villages and an abundance of history.

The walks begin with short, flatter routes to get you started. Then, as you work your way through the book, they gradually get more demanding so you can keep pushing yourself to the next level. To give you a guide to the difficulty of each walk, I have graded them in an increasing fitness range of 1 to 3, with Grade 1 walks being the least demanding and Grade 3 walks being the most challenging. The groups are as follows:

Grade 1 – Stroll
Grade 2 – Stride
Grade 3 – Hike

The best way to tackle *Footpaths for Fitness* is to find out which level you are at to start with so you can develop your fitness from there. If you find a particular walk too hard, it may be a good idea to bring yourself back to earlier walks. This will help you gain the fitness and confidence to try the more difficult walk again in the future, and it will also give you much more enjoyment, which is a huge part of what this book is all about. All the walks are enjoyable in their own right, so even if you are at a more advanced stage, try some of the shorter walks to further develop your love for the outdoors and enjoy the Lincolnshire countryside.

I recommend you wear suitable walking shoes or boots for these walks because paths can become muddy after wet weather and proper footwear will have good grip so you're less likely to slip. Wear whatever is comfortable, obviously wrapping up warm in winter, and don't forget your waterproofs because it can be grim squelching around outside when you're sopping wet. Some of the paths that are very clear at other times of the year can become quite overgrown in summer, though you shouldn't encounter anything too taxing.

Carrying a healthy snack or picnic is always a good idea, though I do mention places where refreshments are available on the route. Please bear in mind that if you pass pubs on your walk, many will have stopped serving food by 2 pm and will not start again until 6 pm. If you're planning to stop for a meal I would recommend assuming this is the case, or giving them a call before you set off.

If it's hot don't forget sun cream and take plenty of water – even if you're not seriously dehydrated, walking is much more enjoyable when you're fully refreshed.

Although sketch maps are provided it is a good idea to have an Ordnance Survey Landranger map with you to check the route. The walks have starting grid references (GRs) so you know exactly where you need to be. To read these, notice how your Ordnance Survey map is divided into squares. If, for instance your grid reference number is 235312, look at the blue numbers going horizontally (from left to right) on the map. The first two numbers in your grid reference are 23, so find the number 23 from the horizontal numbers. The third number is the distance out of 10 between the numbers 23 and 24 on the map. As the number in this case is 5, your point of reference would be halfway between 23 and 24. The fourth and fifth numbers represent the vertical numbers on the map (from top to bottom). In this case you would find the number 31. The sixth number represents the distance out of 10 between 31 and 32. Here it is 2, so the point of reference will be much nearer to 31 than 32. Where the lines through those points meet horizontally and vertically is the location of your starting grid reference.

Places to park are suggested for each walk in this book. Public transport, where there is a regular service, is also mentioned but may mean a short walk to the start point. Check times of trains and buses before you travel (information available from Traveline on 0870 608 2608, www.traveline.org.uk; or train enquiries 08457 484950, www.nationalrail.co.uk).

I really hope you enjoy tackling these routes and that you get as much pleasure as I did from walking them. They are a sample of the best that Lincolnshire has to offer and I believe they are routes you will want to follow again and again.

Matthew Pike

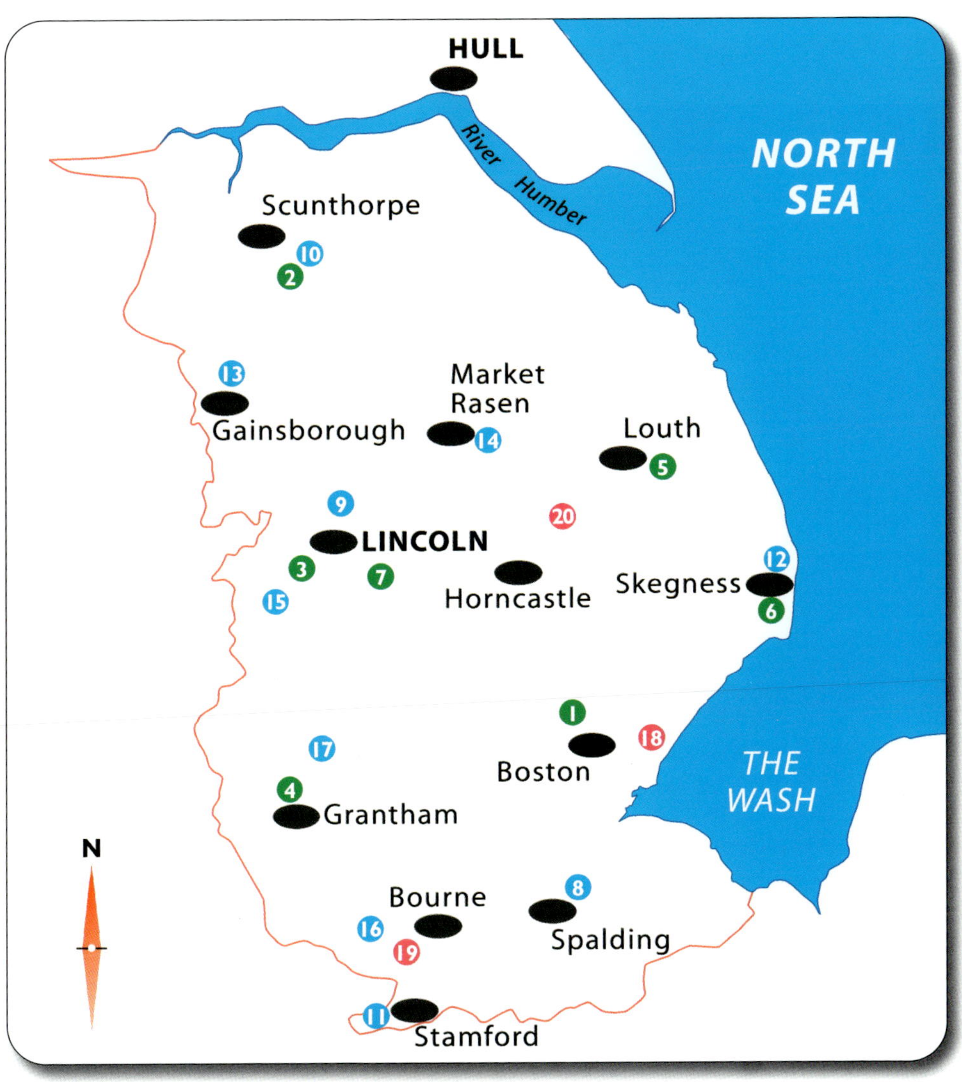

Area map showing location of the walks

Grade 1 – STROLL

Grade 2 – STRIDE

Grade 3 – HIKE

Publisher's Note

We hope that you obtain considerable enjoyment from this book; great care has been taken in its preparation. Although at the time of publication all routes followed public rights of way or permitted paths, diversion orders can be made and permissions withdrawn.

We cannot, of course, be held responsible for such diversion orders and any inaccuracies in the text which result from these or any other changes to the routes nor any damage which might result from walkers trespassing on private property. We are anxious though that all details covering the walks are kept up to date and would therefore welcome information from readers which would be relevant to future editions.

The simple sketch maps that accompany the walks in this book are based on notes made by the author whilst checking out the routes on the ground. They are designed to show you how to reach the start, to point out the main features of the overall circuit and they contain a progression of numbers that relate to the paragraphs of the text.

However, for the benefit of a proper map, we do recommend that you purchase the relevant Ordnance Survey sheet covering your walk. The Ordnance Survey maps are widely available, especially through booksellers and local newsagents.

1 Witham Way Country Park

FOOTPATHS FOR FITNESS

A Perfect Start

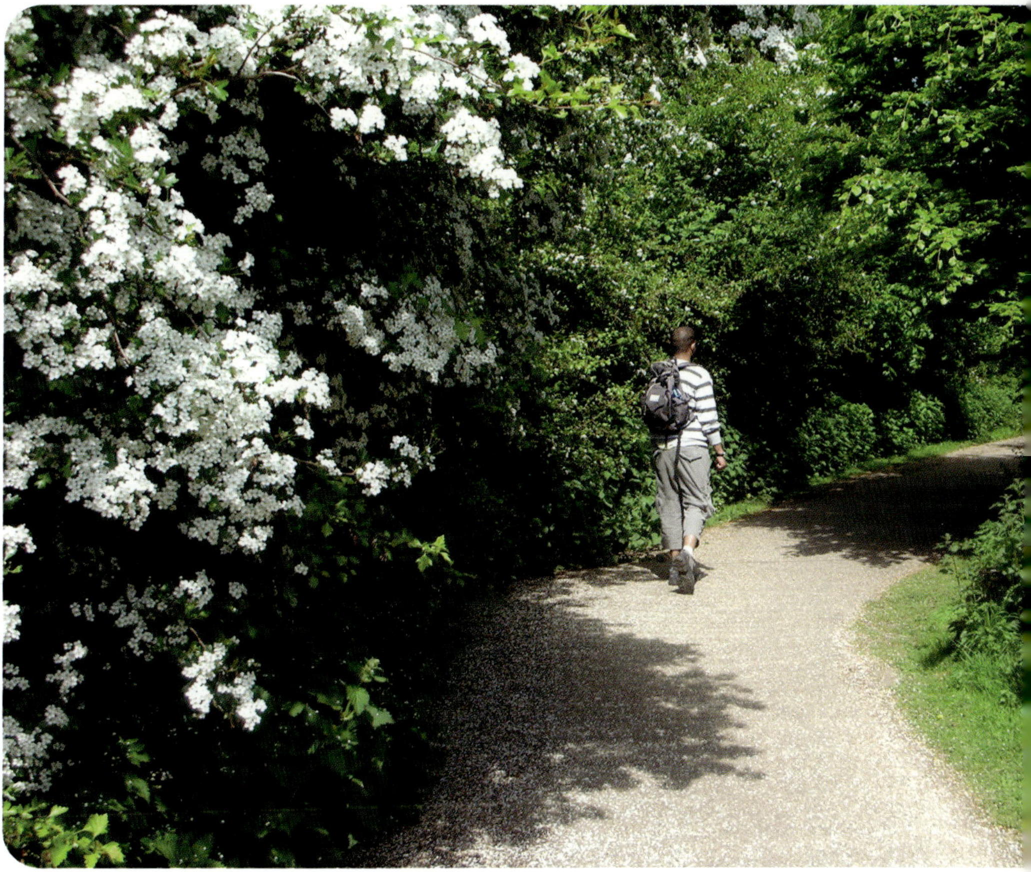

■ *Trees in full bloom in Witham Country Park* ■

This little park, situated just a mile north of **Boston** town centre, is perfect for the new walker starting out on the fitness trail. Not only are there paved paths on flat terrain but it has plenty of benches, a good picnic site and a range of habitats attracting all sorts of wildlife. The wooded areas attract woodpeckers, robins and butterflies, while the **River Witham** provides glimpses of grebes, moorhens and even the odd kingfisher. Walking down the Witham also gives a great view of the **Boston Stump**.

GRADE: 1
ESTIMATED CALORIE BURN: 150

Distance: 1½ miles
Time: 45 minutes
Terrain: Flat with either good or paved paths.
Number of stiles: 0
Starting point: The car park of Witham Way Country Park. GR 318456.
How to get there: From the A16 heading south towards Boston turn right after Kelsey Bridge and go straight over the B1183. Take the next left and the country park is ¾ mile on the right-hand side. Park in the car park there. Buses run from Lincoln to Boston every hour Monday to Saturday and trains from Sleaford and Skegness at least every two hours.
OS map: Landranger 131 Boston & Spalding.
Refreshments: None on the route itself but there is a welcoming picnic site at point 3 of the walk.

The park itself used to be allotments, but they were moved to another part of town and since the early 1990s deciduous trees have been planted on the site, which means the park should become even more attractive as the years pass. If you're keen to make good time in your walks, the flat terrain means you can complete the circuit quickly and burn off those calories.

1 Start by leaving the car park through the main exit and turn right along a road which stops at the gate and becomes a paved cycle path. The football stadium is to your right behind a field, while to your left is a small wooded area. Walk straight ahead, where the path doglegs before reaching a junction. The picnic site is to your left but if you were planning a bite to eat I would recommend waiting until the end of the walk, when you pass the picnic site again. Continue straight on at the junction, where you are now surrounded by trees planted quite recently. The path veers to the right before winding back round to the left. There are several benches along the way here should you need to take a breather. You'll notice that the park has maintained a lot of open space among the trees, making it popular for dog walkers. The path winds its way towards the river, then up the bank where you come to a T-junction. There's an attractive, old-fashioned looking, blue signpost at the top and a tiny garden, with benches immediately to your left.

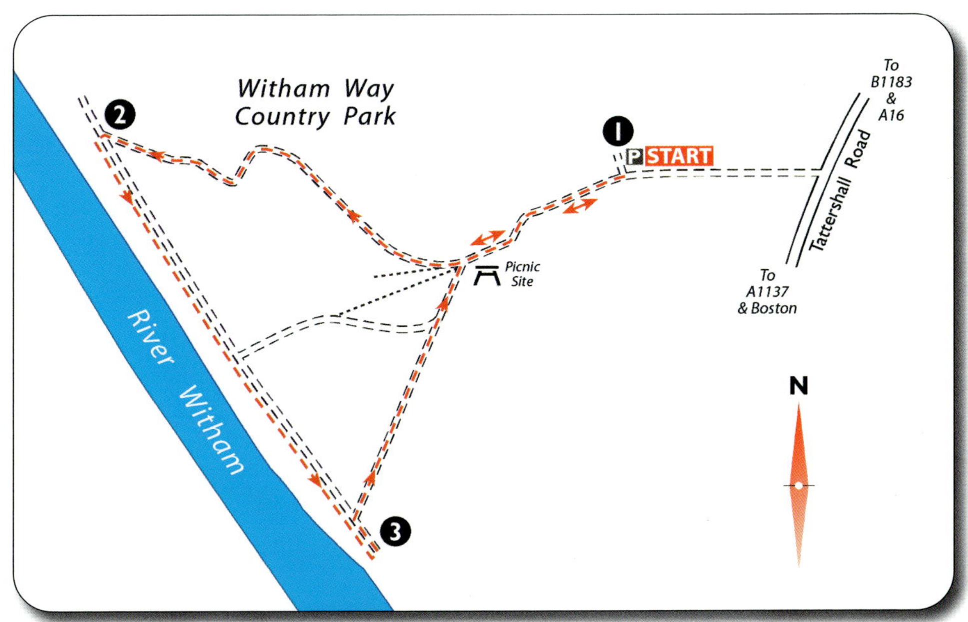

2 Take the small dirt path straight ahead towards the river, then look left for the fantastic sight of **St Botolph's church** – affectionately known as the **Boston Stump** – seemingly rising from the water behind **Grand Sluice** railway bridge. The Stump is more than 272 ft high and is one of the largest parish churches in England. The roof of the tower is higher than that of any non-cathedral church in the world and the building dates back to the 14th century. It can be seen from Lincoln Cathedral and from the Norfolk coast across the water. In years gone by it was a marker post for travellers on the Fens and in the Second World War pilots would use it as a guide back to base. Walk along the grassy river path towards the **Stump**. If you prefer paved paths underfoot, the cycle path runs parallel to the river path all the way down, but doesn't give quite as good a view over the water. This section used to be part of the Boston to Lincoln railway line, which was axed in the 1960s. The trees on your left soon make way for bramble bushes and the path continues for around 900 yards before the paved cycle path takes over. This is the nearest you get to the **Stump** on this walk, so from here you have the best view of all.

3 Turn left along the cycle path so you are walking back in the direction from which you came. There are wooden planks at either side of the track in case you need a break. The bushes to your right are soon replaced by a grass

■ *The firm tracks make for easy walking* ■

field with houses behind. Remain parallel to the river for around 150 yards, where you turn right at the cycle path junction. There is now woodland on either side of you which then opens out to the bramble bushes you saw earlier. Continue along the path and you will eventually see the picnic site on your right. If you're feeling peckish, then this would be the perfect place to stop before continuing to the end. When you reach the next cycle path junction after the picnic site, turn right and this path leads back to the car park.

2 Twigmoor Woods

A Real Gem

FOOTPATHS FOR FITNESS

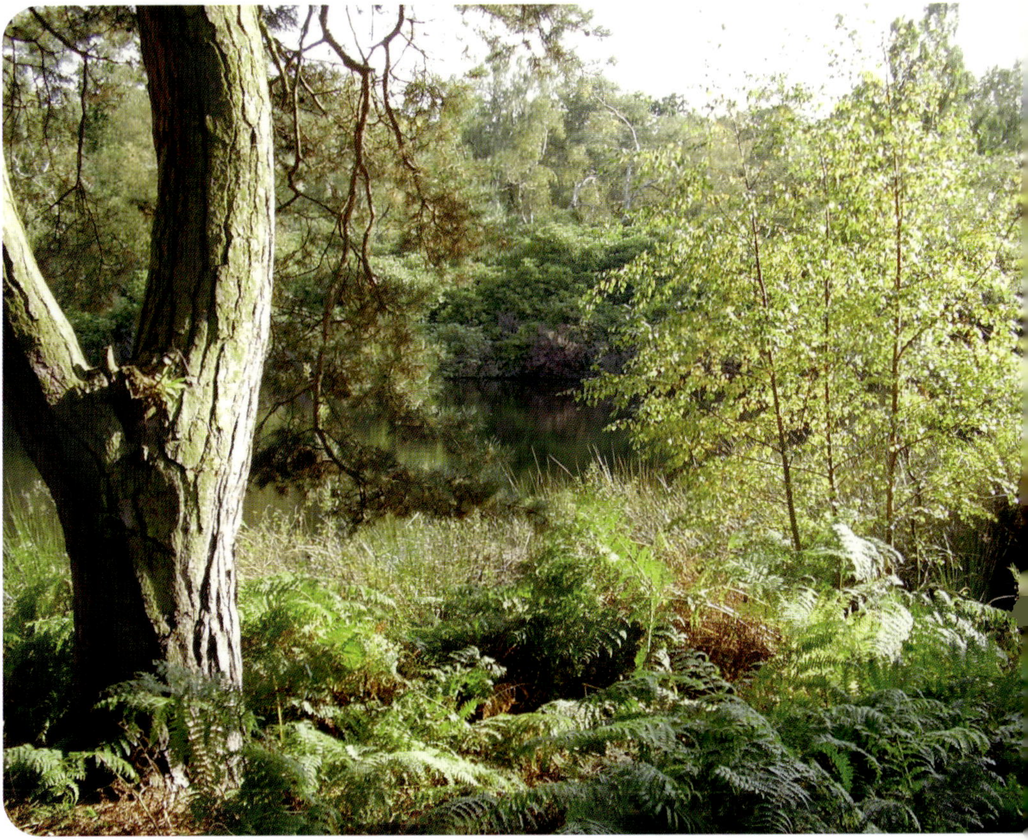

■ *One of the smaller gull ponds in Twigmoor Woods* ■

When the owners of Scawby Estate allowed public access to **Twigmoor Woods** they opened up a real gem. The 130 acre site includes plenty of native woodland as well as introduced conifers and rhododendrons, which are in full bloom during May and early June. Dragonflies love this area in summer and bird lovers can enjoy spotting woodpeckers, buzzards and even the odd nightingale in spring. Dotted among the trees are the **Scawby Gull Ponds**, named after the huge number of black-headed gulls that used to breed there. Today the ponds are

GRADE: 1
ESTIMATED CALORIE BURN: 150

Distance: 1½ miles
Time: 45 minutes
Terrain: Good woodland paths with only a small hill near the end.
Number of stiles: 0
Starting Point: Twigmoor Woods car park. GR 944057.
How to get there: From Scunthorpe take the A18 east, turning right along the B1398. After around 1½ miles Twigmoor Woods car park is on your right.
OS Map: Landranger 112 Scunthorpe & Gainsborough.
Refreshments: None on the route itself but there is a bench ideally situated at point 3 which would make a good place to stop for a picnic.

still abundant with water birds and feature pleasant spots to sit, relax and admire. The walk is short and gentle with numerous benches along the way, should you need a rest. The ground can be a little muddy in places but there are no significant hills to climb and, therefore, it is the perfect follow-up to the first walk, offering a slightly tougher challenge.

1 Leave the car park using the exit opposite the road (next to the sign) and turn right. Continue along this path, with the road running parallel to your right about 30 yards away. The path undulates a little before veering left down a gentle slope. There is a drop to your left but the path instead swings round to the right, passing the first bench on the route. Sections in this area can be a little muddy at times but shouldn't cause too much discomfort. Continue past another bench and you soon reach signposts. Here there is an astonishing looking tree, very gnarled with knobbly branches snaking their way to the top. There is a short cut if you turn left at the signposts but this can be very boggy in places. This route instead takes you straight on for another 20 yards.

2 When you reach the next signposts turn left, following the arrow towards **Gull Ponds**. Follow the path between bushes to a more open area where there is a bench conveniently positioned in a shady spot. Ignore the path heading off to the right and continue along the main path, crossing a tiny stream after which there is a bench on your left. The path curves around a tree-covered mound to the left. Continue straight on at the next set of signposts. The ground here is very comfortable to walk on, with just the

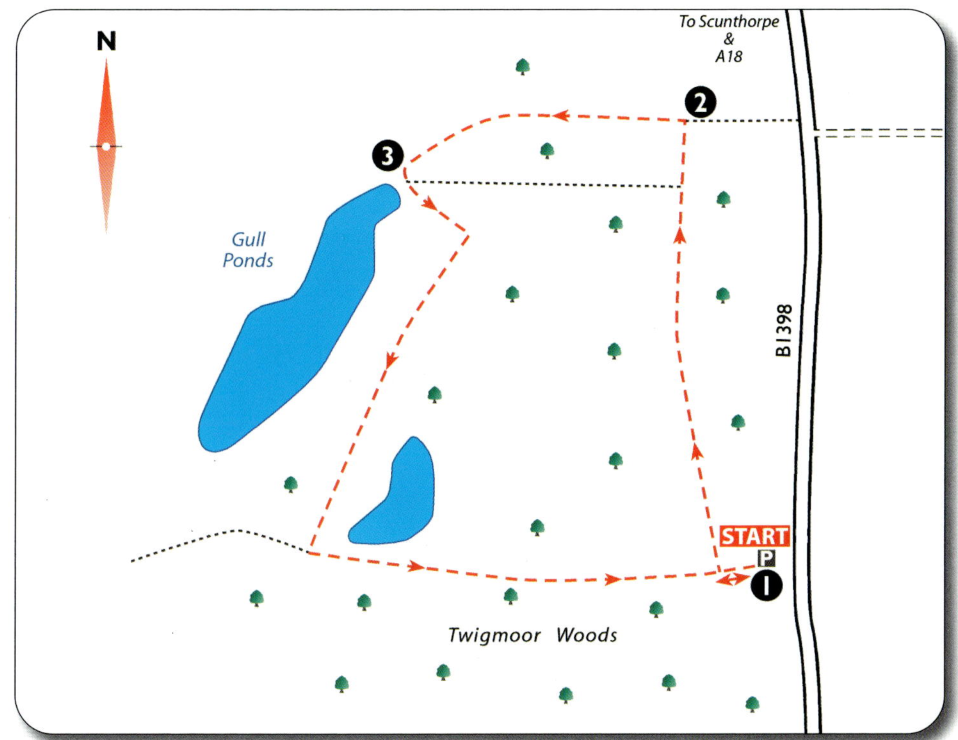

odd pine cone to watch out for. After around 30 yards you reach a point where two large paths split – one goes straight on and one to the right. Take the one to the right and continue, with hedgerows on either side until you reach the lake, the largest of the gull ponds. There aren't so many gulls here now but there are plenty of geese and ducks on the water. This is one of the only spots with a gap, giving a wonderful view across the lake. The bench overlooking the water makes it ideal for a picnic stop. There are also two seats here that have been carved out of tree trunks, though the one on the right is not recommended for anyone with a back problem!

3 Continue along the path as it swings around to the left until you reach a bench at a T-junction of paths. Turn right, where you can see a reedy pond between the trees to your left. You cross what can be a muddy patch. You can turn left here to explore the pond further if you wish, but the walk continues straight on between large bushes and trees. When you reach the 'Private' sign, turn left and a few yards later a bench overlooks the reedy pond, which could make another good picnic spot. The path continues to

■ *Admiring the gull ponds* ■

wind its way through the bushes. Ignore any smaller paths leading off to the left. After another 250 yards you reach another bench to your right and, facing the bench on the opposite side of the path, a seat carved from a tree trunk. The path takes you up a slope raising the heartbeat a little, but when you reach the top you can enjoy the final descent around the bushes to the right where you can now see the car park in front once more.

3 The South Common Walk

A Bird's Eye View

■ *The view over the common* ■

Of the three commons within Lincoln's** boundary, the **South Common** is my favourite because it provides one of the best views of the city. I can't imagine a better vantage point for seeing so many of Lincoln's landmarks than the ridge at the top of the common. From here you can spy the cathedral, the castle, the old water tower, the university, the football stadium and even the **Lincolnshire Wolds** on a clear day. The views are especially stunning in the early morning or evening sunshine when the shadows add depth to the delightful setting. Walkers will also enjoy the wild nature of the common itself. Unlike most city parks, areas of the grass, trees and bushes are left to grow as they please, creating a magnet for birds and wild flowers. The hill you climb during this walk makes this a good test of fitness. If you conquer it comfortably, then you are ready for the Grade 2 walks.

1 The walk begins at **South Park**, a street that could be the setting for an old children's storybook. Grand houses here date from Victorian times and look across the quiet street to the common. Opposite the last house you reach, coming from **Canwick Road**, is a small gate, which is the starting point. Take the larger path that forks to the right, cross straight over the main path and take the next track right. When you continue, you should pass a lone tree on the right. The track takes you along the bottom of the common, where to your right is a bridge crossing a disused railway line and to the left is the hill with a long line of trees at the top. This section of the walk is on bumpy grass tracks and watch for boggy areas. There are many tracks leading left or right up the hill or towards the road but this walk continues straight on for the first section.

After around 250 yards there's a pool to your left enclosed by a wooden fence and trees, which is popular for ducks and moorhens. To the right you can see allotments as well as the prominent spire of the old **Priory church**. You pass another enclosed pool to the left, which may also be worth exploring for a while. When you have just passed the second pool you meet

GRADE: 1
ESTIMATED CALORIE BURN: 160

Distance: 2 miles
Time: 1 hour
Terrain: Mainly grassy tracks with some boggy areas. The ground undulates and there is one hill.
Number of stiles: 2
Starting Point: South Park, Lincoln. GR 977698.
How to get there: From the Lincoln bypass take the A1434 through North Hykeham up to the South Park roundabout. Turn right here, turn right at the end of the road into Canwick Road, the B1188, and take the first right to South Park, parking close to the last house on your right. Regular buses run to Canwick Road from Lincoln city bus station.
OS map: Landranger 121 Lincoln & Newark-on-Trent.
Refreshments: None passed on the actual route but there are plenty of pubs/cafés in Lincoln itself, of course. Alternatively, you could pack a picnic and stop for a rest once you are on the Viking Way (point 2 of the route).

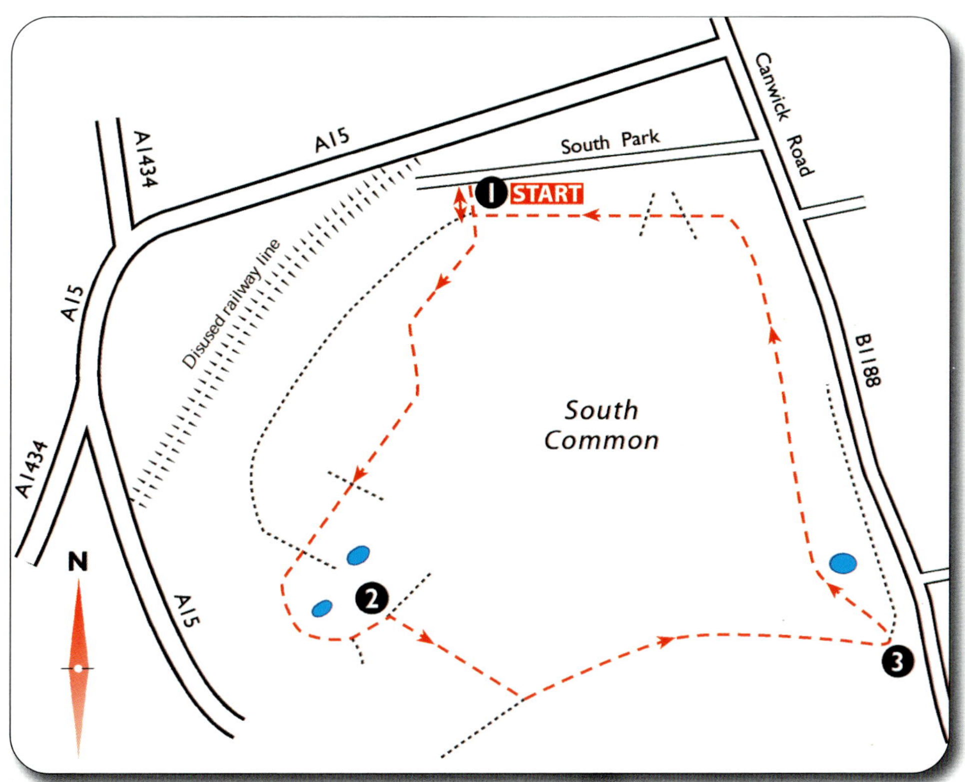

a much bigger path. Take it left towards the hill, passing the same pond again to your left. Follow this path around the back of the pond until it swings left so that you're walking in the direction from which you came.

After around 50 yards a small path heads sharp right straight up the hill. You can see it leading to a small gap just to the left of two very tall trees at the top. This is the only uphill section of the walk so take it bit by bit. Once you have climbed the steep bank in front of the trees, admire the panoramic view. To the left is the south of the city and **North Hykeham**. You can also see the **Swanpool** area, three distant power stations and even some hills in **Nottinghamshire** on a clear day. To the right is **Lincoln** itself with the **cathedral** sitting proudly on the hill. Continue straight up the concrete steps surrounded by wooden fencing to the path at the top. That's the hard part done. There are no more significant hills to climb for the remainder of the route. Once at the top a track, which is part of the **Viking Way**, takes you left across the ridge of the **South Common**. The track is well used but can be slippery after rain and there is often a steep slope down to your left so take care. After 200 yards or so is the first bench. The view here is partially blocked by bushes but it's a good place to rest after your climb. Shortly after this there is a second bench, but it's worth continuing to the final bench for the best view of the lot. From here you feel like a bird looking down on the hustle and bustle of city life. There is no vegetation blocking the way now so you look first to the **South Common** itself, then to the beige, cream, brown and blue houses of **South Park**, to the residential area behind and finally to the old town with the centre-piece that is **Lincoln Cathedral** on the horizon.

■ *Horses run free over the common* ■

3 The path curves round to the left before reaching the road. On the curve, climb over the two stiles to your left and start to descend the hill along the small path. This is an excellent part of the walk to gather pace and to keep the heart pumping at a good rate until the finish. The path leads down a ridge, past a small pond to the right, past two windswept trees that tower over you to the left, and then swings round to the left at the bottom of the hill. The track continues parallel to **South Park**. When you reach the last house at the end of the street, branch off to the gate on the right, finishing this delightful little walk.

 4 Londonthorpe

Stepping up a Gear

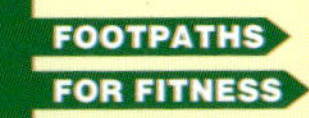

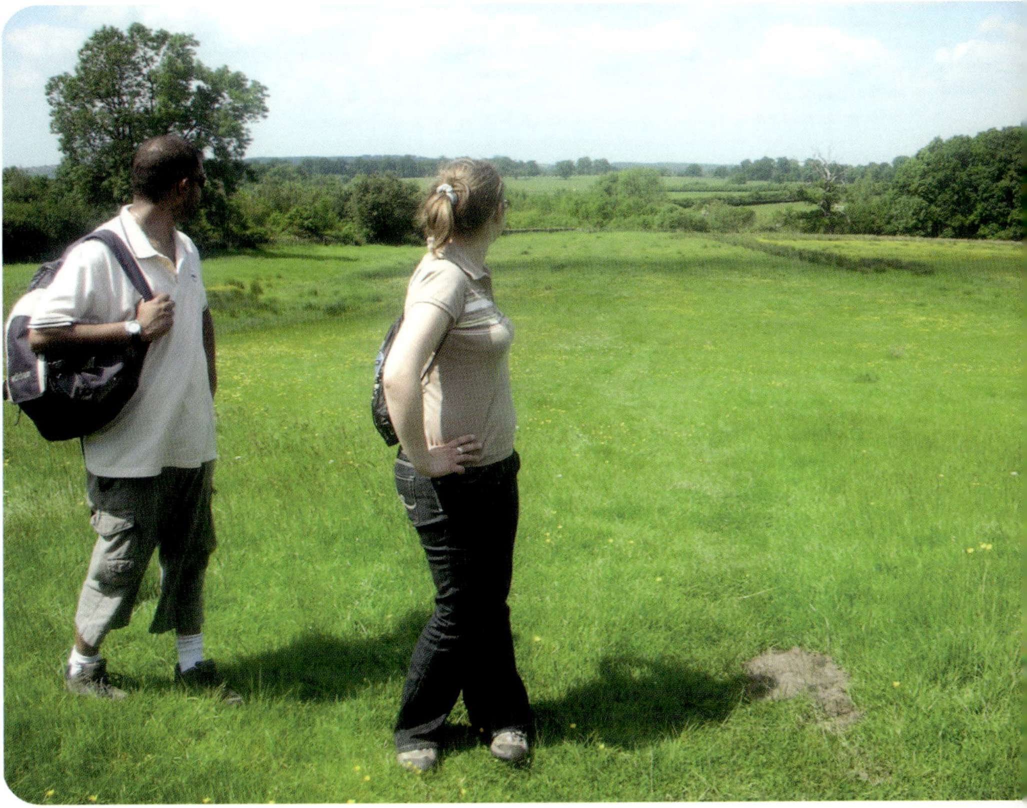

■ *Looking back towards Belton* ■

This is a great walk to aid your fitness development because the small hill and the often uneven terrain make it a little tougher than the previous walks in the book. But it is still a short distance and if you have managed the previous walks comfortably there is no reason why you can't conquer this with gusto. The setting is gorgeous, beginning right next to the grounds of **Belton Hall**. Then, the hill takes you to the tiny but grand village of **Londonthorpe**, which has remained unspoilt and contains some impressive buildings. Finally you walk back down the hill through **Londonthorpe Wood**. This is a project started in the early 1990s by the

> **GRADE: 1**
> **ESTIMATED CALORIE BURN: 160**
>
> **Distance:** 2 miles
> **Time:** 1 hour
> **Terrain:** Mostly along grass fields and dirt tracks – it can be muddy in places. There is one climb leading towards Londonthorpe.
> **Number of stiles:** 4
> **Starting Point:** The car park in Londonthorpe Wood. GR 945379.
> **How to get there:** From the centre of Grantham start taking the A607 north, turning right along Belton Lane. Follow the road right as it becomes Londonthorpe Lane. Continue out of town, take the first road left and park in the car park on your left-hand side.
> **OS map:** Landranger 130 Grantham, Sleaford & Bourne.
> **Refreshments:** None on the route itself so pack a picnic to enjoy at point 2 of the walk.

Woodland Trust to cover nearly 60 hectares with mostly broadleaved species, in particular oak and ash. The walk provides lovely views over **Belton Park** and is conveniently situated just north of **Grantham**.

1 Leave the car park at the main exit and turn left to walk along the tiny lane. There are quite newly planted trees to your left mixed with open fields and marshy areas. To your right, behind the hedge, is a small hill with trees at the top. After the lane crosses a stream look for the footpath sign right, opposite the group of tall trees. Climb over the stile and walk through the grass field. The path here is not always clear so aim for the far right corner. The ground is bumpy underfoot but there is no hill just yet. Shortly before reaching the far corner you will see a stile in the fence to your right with a yellow arrow on it. Climb that one, ignoring the other stile in the corner. If you need a rest the stile can be used as a seat.

Follow the mown path through the long grass, which takes you left. Then continue straight on with bushes on either side. Where the path splits in two take the left fork, which leads straight on. You will soon reach a stile with a mostly dead tree behind it. The tree is so gnarled, especially in winter when there are no leaves, that it could feature in the setting of a horror movie. After crossing the stile, turn 45° to the right and aim for a stile in a gap in the hedge halfway up the hill. The direction you take should be just right of the church at the top of the hill. The ground here is again quite bumpy and there are boggy areas to your left. When you reach the stile continue through the second grass field, aiming just to the right of the red-roofed building towards a green gate in the far right-hand corner.

2 Once through the gate you are now in **Londonthorpe**. This little place is worth exploring, with many large grey-brick houses. The church of St John the Baptist looks unusual, as the tower has a triangular roof. Even the bus stop is impressive, looking more like a monument than a place to sit and wait for public transport. If you need a rest here, there are benches near to the church. From the green gate, cross the main road and continue straight on along **Newgate Lane**. After the last house on your right, take the track to the right which heads straight towards the woods. Keep looking right here because on a clear day you may just get a glimpse of **Belton House** itself. A bench situated part of the way down this track is the perfect spot to have a picnic. It gives you a wonderful view over **Belton Park**. The track cuts between two hedges before reaching **Alma Wood**. Just as you reach it, the path splits into two. Take the left fork, which takes you at first to the left of the trees next to a field, then through the middle of the wood. This mature woodland was planted in the 1850s in memory of the Crimean War and named after one of the battles.

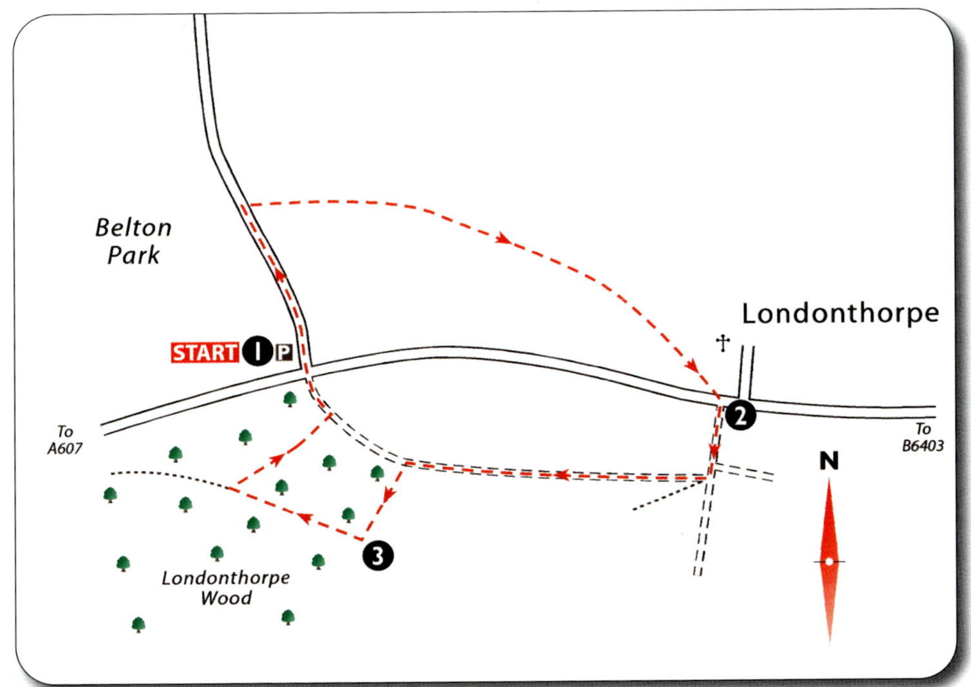

■ A rather grand bus stop in Londonthorpe ■

3 When in the woods take the second, small, unmarked path to the right. This will give you a chance to enjoy the elevated view of the deer park, the lake and scattered woodland one last time. Follow the wide path downhill between the newly planted trees. A little way down there are three stools in case you need another break. Follow the main path downhill – be careful here because it can be slippery and muddy at times. When you are almost at the bottom of the hill, you will reach a junction of paths surrounding a large triangle of grass. Turn right, and follow this path as it meanders through the wood. Eventually you reach a track. Turn left, cross the road and continue down the small lane straight ahead which leads back to the car park.

5 Legbourne to Little Cawthorpe

Stiles Aplenty

FOOTPATHS FOR FITNESS

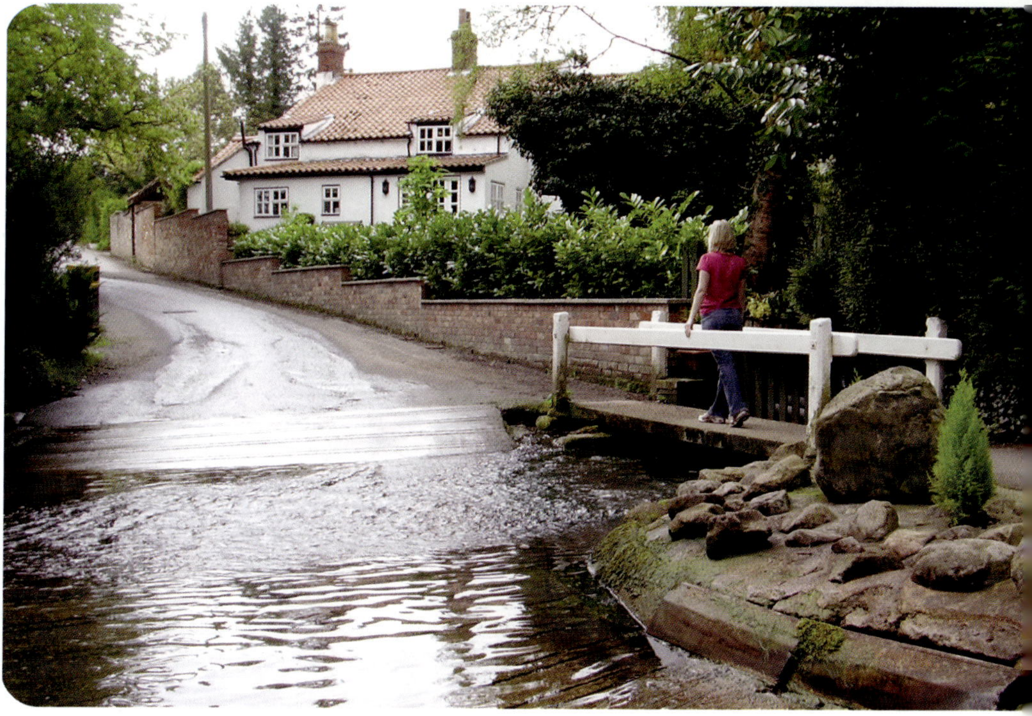

■ *Little Cawthorpe ford* ■

This delightful little walk takes you through one of the prettiest villages in the whole county. **Little Cawthorpe**, with its distinctive cottages, famous ford and glistening pond, makes this stroll on the edge of the **Lincolnshire Wolds** one to remember. There are quite a number of stiles to climb but most of these are in the first half of the walk, along with the bulk of uneven and potentially muddy paths. The second half of the walk is easier under foot and more relaxing.

1 The journey starts in the centre of **Legbourne**, where the post office also contains a shop from which you can purchase last-minute supplies. From here, cross the road towards the field opposite and turn right. Then, almost immediately, turn left down **Mill Lane**. Follow this road for around 600

GRADE: 1
ESTIMATED CALORIE BURN: 160

Distance: 2 miles
Time: 1 hour
Terrain: Partly paved tracks and roads and partly grass paths, sometimes boggy in places.
Number of stiles: 10
Starting point: Legbourne. GR 367844.
How to get there: From Louth take the A157 towards Mablethorpe and park outside the village shop and post office in Legbourne. Four buses per day stop each way between Louth and Mablethorpe.
OS map: Landranger 122 Skegness & Horncastle.
Refreshments: Legbourne has a village shop and the Queen's Head inn (tel. 01507 603839). Little Cawthorpe also has a pub, the Royal Oak, that serves food (tel. 01507 600750).

yards over a hump, across a stream and past an old water mill and fish farm on your right-hand side. After this point you find yourself in open countryside. Continue for another 200 yards and when you see the footpath sign on your left, follow the path diagonally across a grass field. Ahead you see more beautifully green fields decorating the first hills on the east side of the Wolds. Soon, you cross a small road and continue over two stiles and through a paddock. Walk alongside the tall hedge on the left to the next stile. Be careful because this section can become very muddy after rain. The path runs diagonally to the left through the next grass field to another stile, passing on the way a lone tree standing in the middle.

After leaving this field the path takes you right over a double stile and straight through a field, to another stile which then leads to the final field. Climb a gradual slope, walking diagonally left towards a stile situated next to the gate. You have reached the road and after this point there are no more hills to climb and most of the walk is on surfaced paths. The stile makes a handy seat if you need a short break. Otherwise it's time to stamp the mud off your boots and crack on with the journey.

2 Turn right, where a beautiful leafy canopy leads downhill into **Little Cawthorpe**. After passing the **Old Rectory**, walk down **Watery Lane**, the first road on your right. To your left is the small red-brick St Helen's church, standing proudly on top of a mound. The church was closed in 1996 for fears it had become structurally unsound, but has since been in the care of the Churches Conservation Trust, which has repaired the building. Further on is the charming village pond overlooked by a thatched cottage. This is one of two spots in the village perfect for a picnic. A bench alongside the pond, under a willow tree, is ideally placed to enjoy the scene and the birdlife on the water. The pond itself used to be a spring from which the villagers collected their water, but piped water put the spring out of use so it was dammed up to create the village pond. The lane continues, winding between cottages, with hedgerows either side. After a few hundred yards you reach the **Royal Oak**, one of many pubs named after King Charles II who, during the Civil War, supposedly hid in an oak tree to save himself from being captured. However, the pub is more commonly known as 'The Splash' after the ford situated next to the premises.

Luckily you don't have to get your feet wet in crossing the ford because a footbridge has been conveniently placed to one side. While crossing, look left to see a lovely garden windmill rotating in the running water. At the other side of the stream is the **Watering Stone**. This ancient rock used to be situated at the site of the old spring and the villagers would stand on it to collect their water. After being dredged up and placed in someone's garden, it was decided the stone should instead be put on show for all to see. The path takes you around to the right where you follow the very

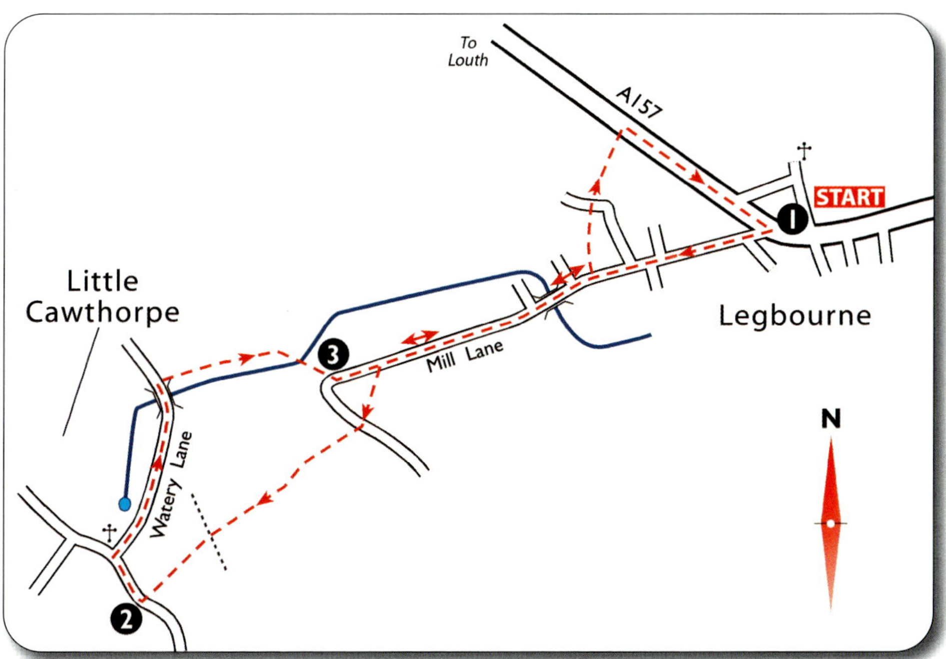

■ *In Legbourne village* ■

shallow stream running alongside to the right. Notice the house to the left which looks like it's straight from the deep south of the United States. Further on to the left is a bench, which is an equally pleasant place to stop for a picnic.

3 Cross the stream again over a small stone bridge, where you reach the road, then turn left at a small roundabout. Follow the road, along which you trekked in the opposite direction at the start of the walk, past the fish farm and watermill. Over the hump in the road is a stile to your left. If you've had enough of stiles for one day then the road continues straight back to the start. But if you want more, the stile takes you to a path that leads across the centre of a small paddock. It veers off to the right behind a red-brick barn and through a small gap in a tall hedge, where you climb your final stile. The path continues between a wall to the left and a fence to the right, straight over a street and between two more fences until you reach the main road. Follow the pavement on the right-hand side of the road, which veers to the right before curving back to the left and you have reached the end of this little adventure.

6 Gibraltar Point

A Haven for Birds

■ Above Shoveller's Pond ■

Believe it or not, what is now this wonderful and hugely important nature reserve nearly became a speedway track. This was one of the proposed ideas when the port that once stood here silted up, forcing the site out of use. These days the 430 hectares of sand dunes, seashore and the ever rarer salt marshes provide vital habitat for a wide range of migrating birds and resident waders. Little terns breed here, as do ringed plovers and whitethroat. Of the migrants, the reserve once hosted a flock of 30,000 swallows. Cowslips and pyramidal orchids are among the many wildflowers found here and look also for the reintroduced colony of natterjack toads. The series of footpaths make it a fantastic place to walk whether you have an interest in the wildlife or not. Its remote location means you can wander happily without hearing a motor vehicle and you can always find a quiet corner to yourself. The paths are very well maintained and there are benches at regular intervals.

1 Take the main entrance into the reserve from the car park along the paved path, next to the information board. You soon pass a pond on the left where you can occasionally spot the blue flash of a kingfisher if you're lucky. In this section there is bush land either side and after around 100 yards you reach the **Mere Hide** to your left, looking out over another lagoon. The path ceases to be paved and becomes a well maintained dirt track. You pass livestock fields to your left and cross several streams. A path right leads to hides looking over several ponds, some of which are freshwater and others are saltwater. But this route follows the main path, straight on past a small lagoon to your left with a bench on the right-hand side. The path veers gradually right, passing a small pond to your right, before winding round to the left where you will see a board with a map of the reserve on it.

Follow the grass path left through the gate and straight on, with shrubs on your left and grassy dunes to the right. There is a good chance you will also see a flock of Hebridean sheep, introduced here to nip the shrubs back and stop them from invading the dunes, and you may pass a herd of small Dexter cattle along this section. After around 300 yards you will see wooden steps going left up the side of a bank. They lead to a bench giving a beautiful view over **Shoveler's Pond**, which can become almost hidden in reeds during the summer months. In spring a cuckoo often lays her eggs in a warbler's nest in the reeds here. This is a great place to sit and relax hearing nothing but the birds and the distant sea behind you.

GRADE: 1
ESTIMATED CALORIE BURN: 180

Distance: 2½ miles
Time: 1¼ hours
Terrain: Flat with mostly good sandy paths.
Number of stiles: 0
Starting point: The car park at Gibraltar Point nature reserve. GR 558589.
How to get there: From the centre of Skegness, head south along Drummond Road, which soon becomes Gibraltar Road. Park in the first car park on the left-hand side once you have entered the nature reserve. There is a parking charge and proceeds go to the upkeep of the reserve.
OS map: Landranger 122 Skegness & Horncastle.
Refreshments: None on the route itself so pack a picnic to enjoy at point 2 of the walk.

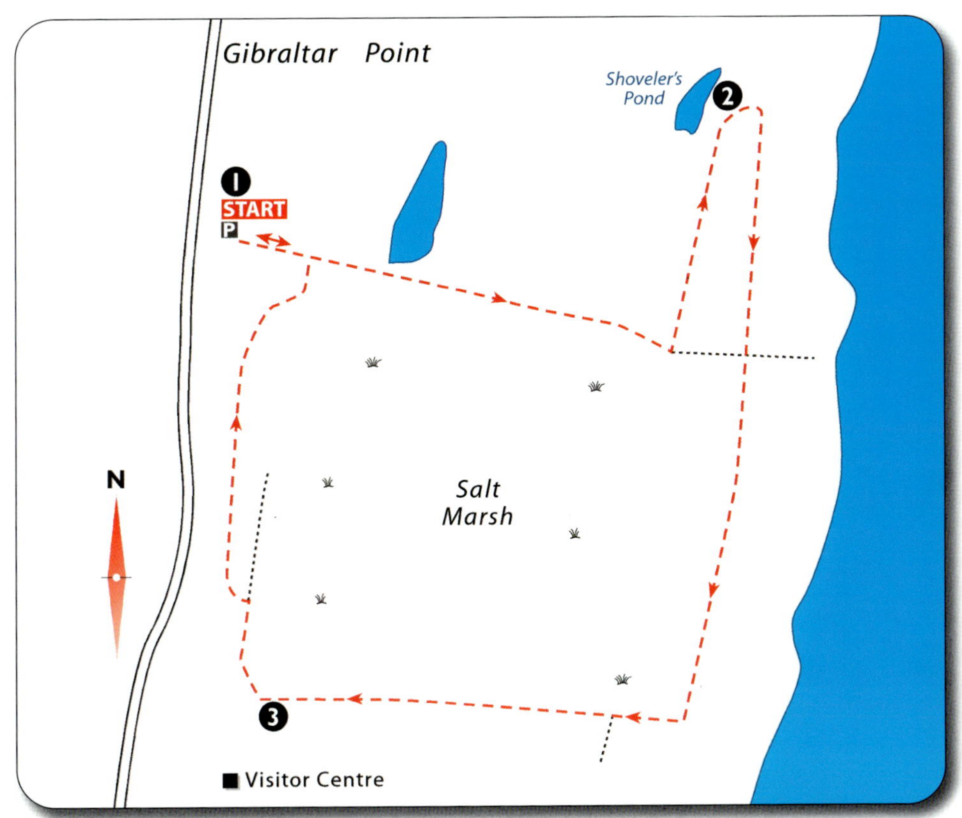

2 Continue straight on, turn right walking down the steps and take a left. When you reach the open area there is a choice of paths. Turn right so that the sea is now on your left-hand side. Continue along this grass path for another 400 yards until you reach the gate. Here you can see the **North Sea** to your left-hand side. Go through the gate and it's really worth taking the steps up **Mill Hill** to your right for a great view over the whole reserve. This is the highest point and from the top you can see the shrubs, fields, lagoons and salt marsh around you. To the east is the **North Sea** with the wind farms and on a clear day you can see **Norfolk**. You may even see seals lying on the sand dunes uncovered at low tide from this point. To the west you can see as far as the **Lincolnshire Wolds** when the weather's fine.

When you have finished admiring the view, walk down the steps, turn right at the bottom then turn left towards the gate. Follow the well maintained stony track straight on, with the bank to your right and the sea out of sight behind dunes to your left. Eventually you reach another gate at

■ *The Hebridean sheep keep the rosebay willow herb under control* ■

a T-junction. Go through the gate, ignore the path heading towards the sea and instead turn right. This track leads slightly downhill from between the banks to a great view across the flat salt marshes and its lagoons. There is a bench here on the left which would make a good picnic spot. The path becomes paved and cuts straight through the marsh. At the highest tides the sea will encroach this far. After crossing a stream shortly before the visitor's centre car park, take a right along a grassy path which runs in front of a bench also looking out over the salt marsh.

3 The path continues along the edge of the plain with a bank and a Second World War pillbox to your left. After around 150 yards you reach a bench. Then, 50 or so yards beyond this, a small grass path leads up the side of the bank towards the wooded area. This can be overgrown at times. When you reach the dip in the group of trees, turn right so you're walking parallel to the road on your left in the same direction as before. This wide grass track runs at first between the trees, then the trees become smaller and more sporadic. When you reach the fence, continue straight on with the fence on your right. Here, you can see the full range of woodland birds, gulls and waders. Pass a small lagoon to your left, and follow the fence around to the right before the path breaks off to the left and reaches the main paved path you walked along at the start. When you reach it, turn left and the path leads back to the car park.

Chambers Farm Wood
A Wildlife Paradise

■ A small pond at point 3 of the walk ■

With its ancient trees, large collection of native butterflies and a dawn chorus to die for, **Chambers Farm Wood** is a wildlife paradise. Visit at the right time of year and you could be treated to the sight of luminous glow worms, or to the sound of a nightingale in full voice. The wood is the most visited of the ancient lime woods in the area and many who come here find it a peaceful and relaxing place situated in a very rural spot. The national nature reserve is a mixture of medieval forest and trees planted on former agricultural land. The walk begins along one of the main trails on a good track, passing the ancient **Hatton Wood** along the way. Then the route takes you off the beaten track to the more remote parts of the wood before returning to the car park once more. The second part of the walk is the real test of your stamina because it can be quite muddy but there are no hills to worry about in the woods.

1 Facing away from the picnic site, turn right past the green gate along the well maintained track. This is a section of the wood where conservationists have attempted to reintroduce the nearly extinct dormouse. Ignore the track you soon see to the right and continue past the post with red and white markings, signifying the various trails around the reserve. The track curves to the left and then straightens for a long period. The trees around here are being managed for timber and the track is wide to allow for the 40-ton timber trucks to access the woodland when it's time for collection. Continue straight across the track crossroads, noting that the marker posts now only

GRADE: 1
ESTIMATED CALORIE BURN: 180

Distance: 2½ miles
Time: 1¼ hours
Terrain: Good tracks to start with, then grassy tracks which can become boggy at times and a little overgrown in summer.
Number of stiles: 0
Starting point: The car park at Chambers Farm Wood. GR 148739.
How to get there: From Lincoln take the A158 east to Wragby. At the traffic lights turn right along the B1202 and after around 3 miles turn left into Chambers Farm Wood.
OS map: Landranger 121 Lincoln & Newark-on-Trent.
Refreshments: None on the route itself so pack a picnic to enjoy halfway round the walk.

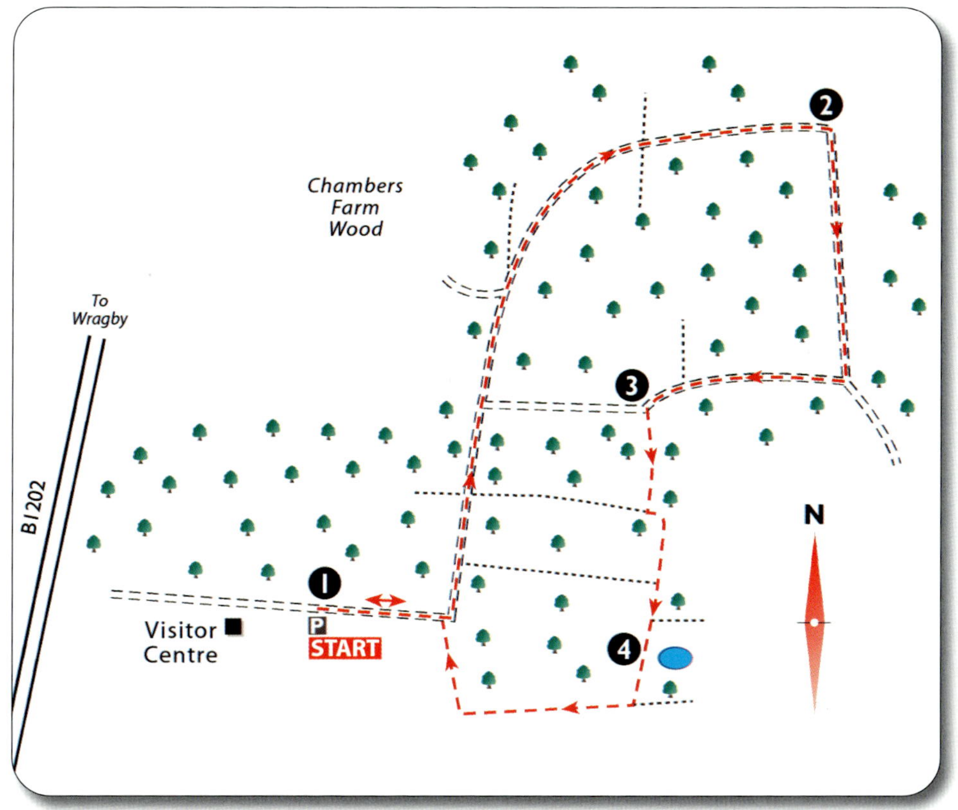

mark the red trail. The woodland each side of you is not dense and it is quite easy to spot birds.

Eventually you reach a section where the track swings around to the right. Ignore this and continue along a slightly smaller track straight on, to the left of the bench. There are now largely bushes to the left and deciduous trees to the right with more dense undergrowth than before. Soon you pass several boggy sections to the right with Scots pine trees behind. There are also newly planted trees to the left and plenty of wild flowers here depending on the time of year. Keep to the track as it gradually swings to the right, following the red markers and ignoring the tracks deviating left and right as you go. There's a small dyke running to your left and you also pass a boggy area on the left-hand side. When you complete the turn you have the beautiful and ancient **Hatton Wood** to your left. Access to this area of the reserve is minimal and it is a wild stretch of forest. You soon cross a stream and pass the giant lone poplar tree to the right.

■ *Walking briskly towards the finish* ■

2 When you reach the edge of the wood the track swings round 90° to the right. Follow it round so that the ancient **Minting Wood** is to your left. This isn't as dense as **Hatton Wood** and has limited undergrowth. After a couple of hundred yards walking along the straight track, it swings round to the right again. Follow it round, ignoring another track leading straight ahead. As you turn right you'll pass an open triangle of boggy land with bushes and several dead trees in the middle. To the right the trees are very sparsely situated around wetland and there are conifers behind this large open space.

3 The path curves to the left. As it does so, take the path left opposite the post with the red marker (if the track curves back round to the right again, you have gone too far).You will find you are now walking along a track not often ventured in the woods. This track can be soggy and overgrown at times and follows a stream running parallel to your left. The path veers slightly to your right; there are conifers to the left and predominantly silver birch trees to the right. It becomes quite jungle-like and you soon pass a small pond to your left behind the stream. Eventually you reach a footbridge to your left. Cross over the stream but be careful here because you may have to duck under some branches. The path takes you to the edge of the wood and you can see the field ahead.

Follow the path straight on. You are now walking along the edge of the wood – to your left is a field with more woodland beyond it. At the next corner there is an old rotting bench if you need a breather. Follow the narrow path round to the right – there are conifers to your right, a field behind a ditch to your left and bushes either side that you may have to fight your way through a little when they become overgrown. Ignore the path leading right (which is a shortcut should you need it) and continue straight on. The path is not so overgrown with bushes now. When you reach the end of the field cross the ditch and follow the path as it meanders its way through the trees. You soon reach a small lily pond surrounded by trees to your left. It's a beautiful, secluded spot to stop for a picnic, should you want to, mid-walk. There are no benches here but on a dry day there should be plenty of places to sit.

4 The track can be very boggy here. If it's bad, then the edge of the woodland to the right provides slightly higher ground, but rejoin the path as soon as possible, as it continues in the same direction as before. Very soon you'll reach a small path leading right. Follow it as it takes a quick left-right, past a tiny pond to the right and across a stream. Then follow it straight up the lovely grass track which is now refreshingly dry after the boggy land. Turn right when you reach the bigger track. Follow it as it swings round to the left and continue straight on when it rejoins the main track, leading you back to the car park.

Spalding
A Taste of the Fens

■ *St Paul's church seen from across the river* ■

This walk is set just north of the beautiful market town of **Spalding**. Walkers could combine the route with a day in the town itself, with its beautiful Ayscoughee Hall and the relaxing water taxi transporting you along Spalding's waterways during the summer months. In spring the town hosts the annual Flower Parade attracting 100,000 visitors. The circuit begins along the picturesque banks of the **River Welland** and continues north until it joins the tiny country lanes that lead back to the start. It's not a long walk and it is very flat, but the lack of benches and places to rest make it a good test of stamina. The flatness of the walk also means you can make good time if you wish to push yourself that little bit further. This level landscape gives you a real feel for the nature of the **Fens**, which you can often see stretching into the distance. If you can complete this route comfortably, you should be ready for longer walks in this section.

1 Start by walking along Marsh Road, which soon becomes Roman Bank, heading towards the town. There is a field to your right and, as you approach the river, you can see the lovely spire of **St Paul's church** to your left. Just before reaching the river, take the footpath right along the right-hand side of the river bank. You are now walking alongside a tidal river and heading away from a dam, also used as a road bridge. Herons are a common sight along here and the keen bird watcher may be able to spot other water birds such as cormorants and shelducks. The **Welland** gradually curves to the right before straightening, with a road bridge crossing the river in the distance ahead and a factory diagonally left on the opposite side of the water. Stay on the river bank itself, ignoring any tracks leading off to the right. To your right are fields, trees and large greenhouses – the latter are a particularly common sight in this part of the county.

GRADE: 2
ESTIMATED CALORIE BURN: 360

Distance: 3½ miles
Time: 1½ hours
Terrain: Completely flat on either small roads or riverside paths.
Number of stiles: 0
Starting point: GR 263243.
How to get there: Heading south along the A16 which bypasses Spalding, turn right along the A151, then first right, continuing past Springfields shopping centre. At the T-junction turn right into Marsh Road and park on the left when the double yellow lines stop. A regular bus service to Springfields shopping centre operates from Spalding town centre.
OS map: Landranger 131 Boston & Spalding.
Refreshments: Springfields shopping centre has a range of cafés.

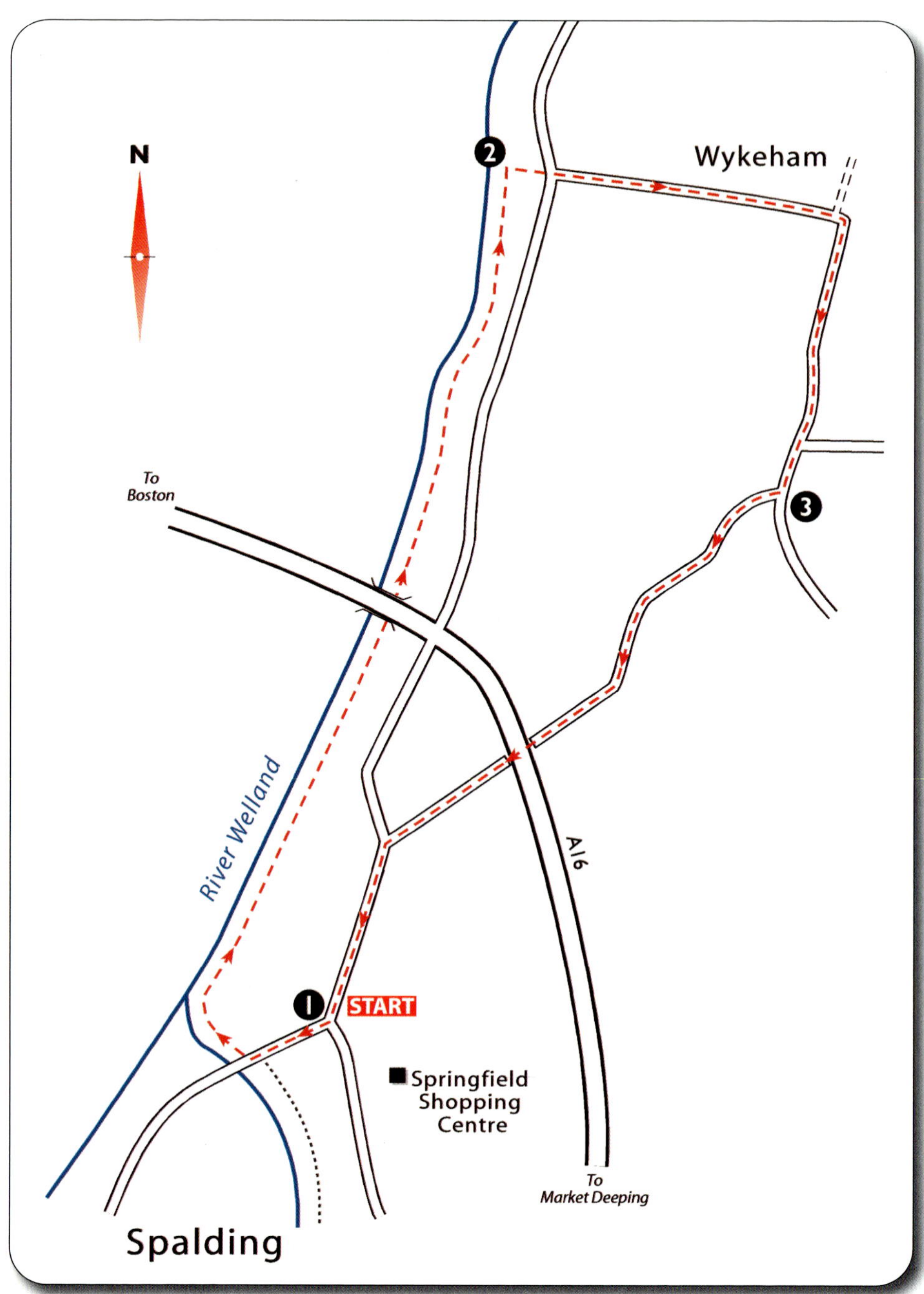
N
Wykeham
To
Boston
River Welland
A16
2
3
1
START
Springfield
Shopping
Centre
To
Market Deeping
Spalding

■ *Quiet lanes are a feature of this route* ■

As you approach the bridge, drop down to the left of the bank so you can walk underneath. Climb the bank again when you reach the other side and continue along the top. You will notice the small lane to your right getting gradually nearer as you progress. Continue through an open gate and follow the river as it bends slightly to the right and back to the left again. To your right are lovely gardens teeming with trees and to your left you can see

Vernatt's Drain behind the **River Welland**, parallel to the path. You go through another open gate before passing an old wooden barn in the small field to your right. The road is running very close to the path behind a field until eventually it meets the bank.

2 Walk to the road down the side of the bank immediately after a gate and a small group of trees to your right. Turn right so that you're walking in almost the opposite direction from which you came. The river is now on your right, behind the bank, and there are fields to your left. Take the first lane to your left. This is a pretty, narrow lane with trees either side. It's quiet along here with very few cars, but cyclists often use it for circular routes from Spalding. The lane crosses a dyke and there are small dykes either side of the road. After around 600 yards you reach a very grand looking house and a farm to your left. There are the remains of an old chapel at this site, though these are not visible from the road itself. Follow the road as it turns sharp right – the trees either side are more sporadic now than before. There are huge fields either side of you and you can see the river bank in the distance on your right.

3 Ignore the lane leading left after around 700 yards and, just before reaching a large electricity pylon, take the lane right 150 yards on. Don't expect to see any vehicles along here as the lane, cut in half by the A16 bypass, essentially leads nowhere. The lane bends left and back to the right again. There are ditches either side with bushes appearing every so often. The lane winds its way towards the main road. A gate leads you to a path up the side of the bank. Cross the main road with care (as cars travel very fast along here) and walk down the path the other side. A gate at the bottom leads you back to the same lane that has been sliced in half. It continues past houses on either side until it reaches a T-junction. Turn left here so there are trees to your right and a large building to the left. The road swings back to the right and to the start once more.

9 Brayford Pool to Boultham Park

In the Heart of the City

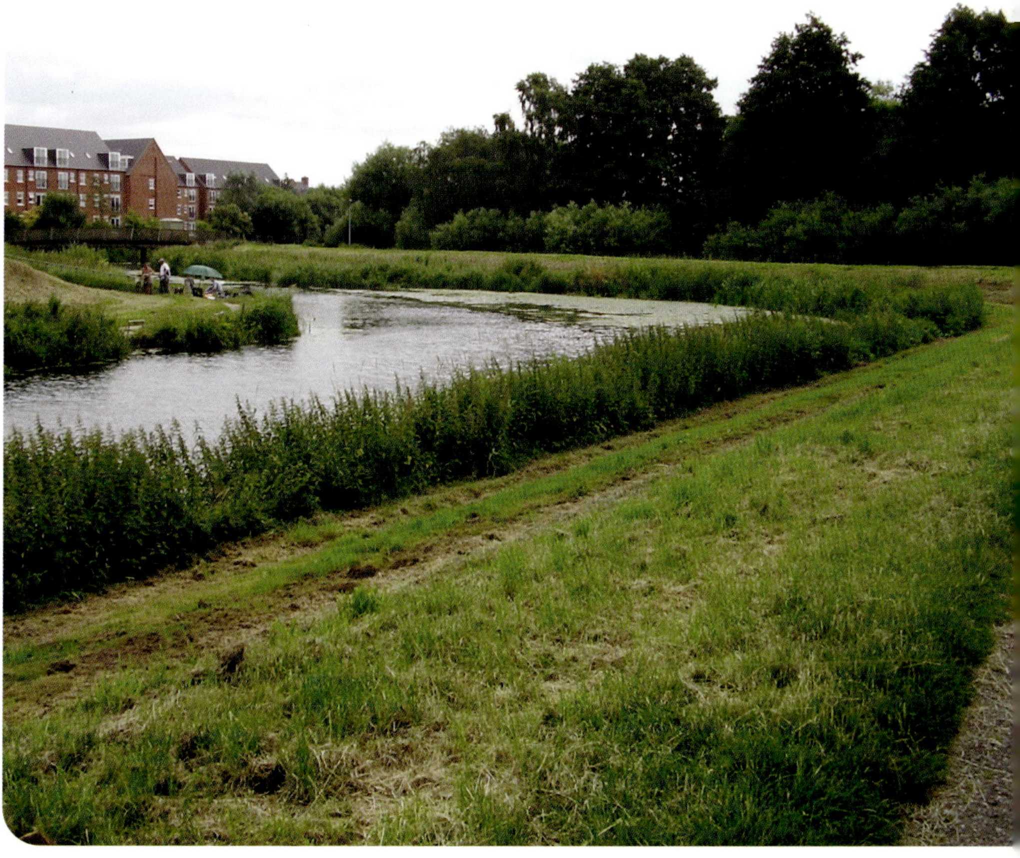

■ *The route beside the River Witham* ■

This **walk is ideal** for those within easy access of Lincoln because it starts right at the heart of the city. Yet it is so tranquil you often forget you're surrounded by urban life. The journey takes you along the gentle **River Witham**, with its abundant birdlife and green weeping

GRADE: 2
ESTIMATED CALORIE BURN: 420

Distance: 4 miles
Estimated Time: 2 hours
Terrain: Flat and mostly on paved footpaths.
Number of stiles: 0
Starting point: Brayford Waterfront, Lincoln. GR 973712.
How to get there: From the Lincoln bypass, heading north, turn right along Carholme Road. At the end turn left, take the first right along Newland and turn right into Lucy Tower Street. If using public transport, turn left from the train station (right from the bus station) along St Mary's Street and straight on to Wigford Way, where a multi-storey car park is situated next to Brayford Pool.
OS map: Landranger 121 Lincoln & Newark-on-Trent.
Refreshments: Two pubs, both serving food, sit next to each other in Newark Road, halfway through the walk, the Plough (tel. 01522 511553) and the Wagon & Horses (tel. 01522 870808). Brayford Pool (at the start and the finish) has an abundance of pubs and restaurants.

willows, and into one of the city's most beautiful parks with its open lawns, enormous trees and popular lake. Throughout much of the route you can enjoy a view of **Lincoln Cathedral** standing proudly on the hill to the north. The circuit is well suited to those in the early stages of their fitness walks because it consists largely of flat, well maintained paths. If you have never walked it before, I'm sure you will be pleasantly surprised by how richly green the area surrounding the river is, especially in summer, and the gentle terrain should make it an enjoyable experience for walkers of any level of fitness.

1 The walk starts at the bustling modern **Brayford waterfront**, on the north side of the pool. Over the last few years the site has been transformed into a series of restaurants and bars, with the university dominating the south side. The water itself is teeming with boats and you cannot fail to spot the huge number of swans gracing the pool. Climb the steps to your left as you face the water, cross the bridge over the east side of the **Brayford pool** and turn immediately right along **Brayford Wharf East**. The view over the water from this road is always impressive, especially at sunset. Continue over the railway line with the river to your right. Follow the path right over the river and cross the **Ropewalk** at the pedestrian crossing. Walk

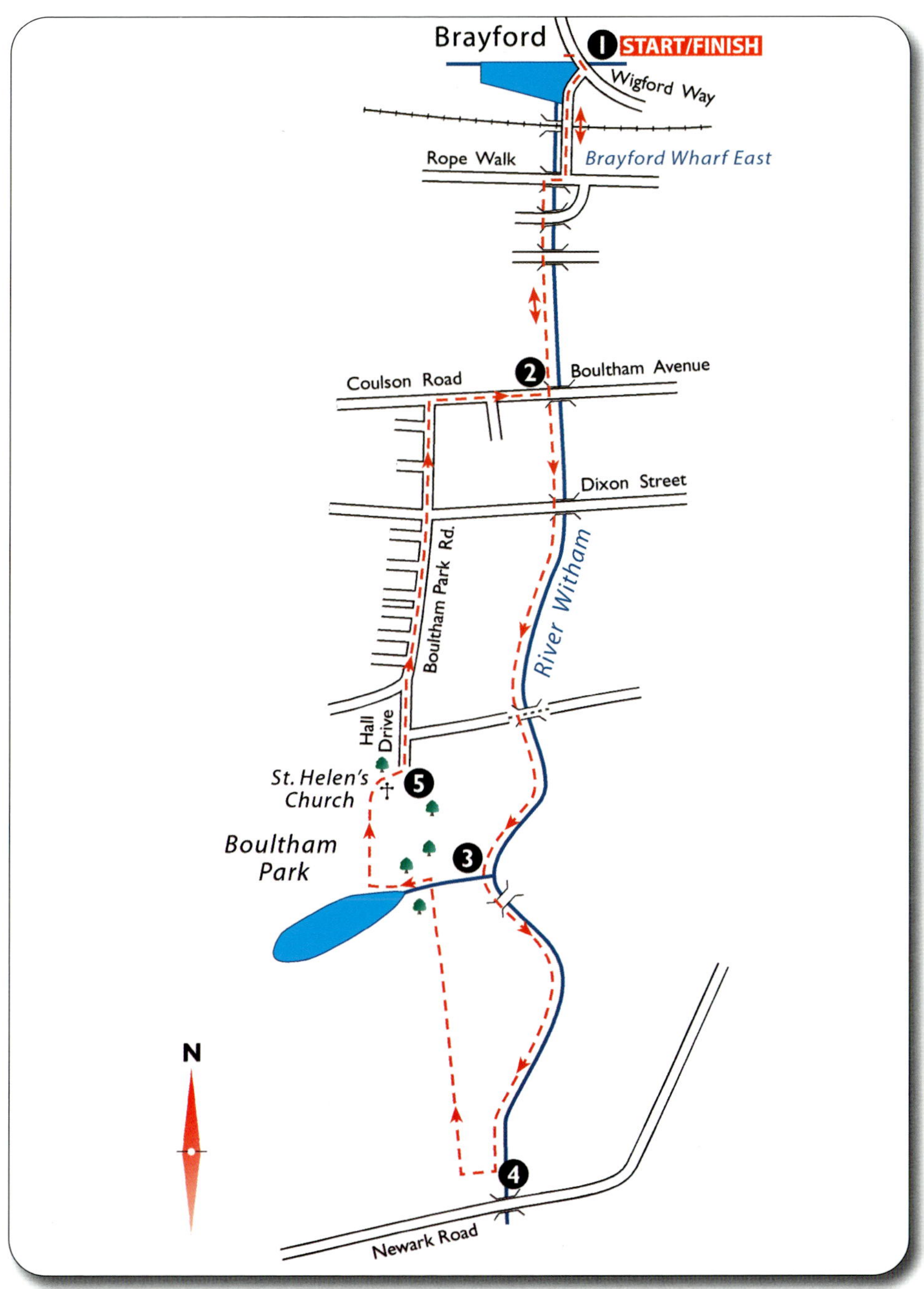

Brayford
START/FINISH
Wigford Way
Brayford Wharf East
Rope Walk
Coulson Road
Boultham Avenue
Dixon Street
Boultham Park Rd.
River Witham
Hall Drive
St. Helen's Church
Boultham Park
Newark Road
N

straight on with the river now on your left-hand side, crossing two more roads so the factory is on your right and residential housing is on your left across the river.

2 After around 500 yards you cross **Boultham Avenue** and then the busy **Dixon Street** over the pedestrian crossing. It is now that you can really start to enjoy the countryside feel while meandering along the river path. The landscape surrounding the river opens out and you walk on a grassy bank with bushes and a smaller stream to the right. You can choose whether to take the smooth cycle path that dips below the height of the river bank or the more crumbly footpath that runs along the top and offers views across the **Witham**. The two paths join at a small bridge, which you cross and follow the cycle path straight on. The path breaks into two once again and you can choose either the footpath or the cycle track. There are plenty of trees towering over the right-hand side of the paths and scores of allotments in the nearby fields.

3 The river curves to the right and joins woodland that leads to **Boultham Park**. Those taking the cycle path route will have to join the footpath here and follow the river as it dog-legs left and right. While on this section it's worth glancing over your shoulder for a particularly special view of the **cathedral**. Pass the footbridge over the river and you will soon see that the woodland on the right clears to become green paddocks with horses grazing in the long grass. Your elevated position gives you a great view over the fields and sometimes the pleasant smell of crisps wafts from the Walkers factory to your left. The footpath continues until **Newark Road**, where there are two pubs next to each other if you fancy halfway refreshments.

4 If you would rather carry on, follow the path that U-turns to the right before you reach **Newark Road**. Here it joins a cycle path taking you back in the direction from which you came. It leads into a deciduous wood, past a 'crossroads' of cycle paths and over a small stream. This is the best part of the walk to spot woodland birdlife and a huge number of grey squirrels. Take the path immediately left after the stream leading into **Boultham Park**. This 20-hectare park was secured as a public facility by Lincoln City Council in 1929. On site are the remains of the hall of the Boultham estate, once owned by the Ellison family. It is now a popular spot for dog walkers, fishermen and youngsters playing football and basketball. There are numerous benches overlooking the lake, offering the best picnic spots of the walk. Follow the path to the right of the lake and take the first right across

The woods leading to Boultham Park

■ *Brayford Waterfront* ■

an open grass field on which you can see a bandstand in the distance to your left. Keep going until you reach the putting and bowling greens and turn right into the wood again, where you pass **St Helen's church**, parts of which date back to the 13th century.

5 The track becomes a road which you follow round to the left and up **Hall Drive** – a street which makes you feel more like you're in a small village than a city. It joins the leafy Boultham Park Road where you continue straight on for around two thirds of a mile – the best place to cross **Dixon Street** being the pedestrian crossing on the left-hand side of **Boultham Park Road**. Continue past what used to be St Matthew's church – a Grade II listed building made from metal which was being converted into a mosque until it burnt down in 2008. Turn right along **Coulson Road**, which becomes **Boultham Avenue**, back towards the river. When you reach the **Witham** turn left so you are travelling north with the river on your right. For the final part of the route, retrace your steps from the start of the walk continuing straight along the river path. Turn right after crossing the **Ropewalk**, over the bridge and along **Wigford Way** with the river now to your left. Cross the bridge over the east side of the **Brayford Pool**, walk down the steps to your left immediately afterwards and you're back on the **Brayford Waterfront** once more.

10 Broughton
Woodland and Open Spaces

■ *In East Wood* ■

This walk takes full advantage of **Broughton**'s position next to many acres of fine woodland. Cooperation between landowners and the Countryside Commission (now Natural England) means there are many paths open to walkers both in the fields surrounding the town and through the trees. The route offers you a good challenge in terms of distance, while providing great variety in the surroundings. Starting in the centre of **Broughton**, it soon frees itself across open fields, through **East Wood** and back to the town again. The woods are blessed with many exotic species of trees, abundant birdlife and, in summer, can be carpeted with wild flowers.

1 The route begins alongside **St Mary's church**, in the middle of town. The building dates back to the 11th century, maybe before, but there have been major alterations since then. Facing the church, turn left along **High Street**. If you need to stock up on picnic goods, you soon pass a convenience store on the left. Follow the road as it bends a little to the left, walk past the **Methodist church** and continue for another 50 yards until you reach **Beck Lane** on your left. Walk along this quiet little lane, with conifer hedgerows on the left, as it leads slightly downhill. Continue straight ahead when the lane bends to the right and, where the road stops, follow the path across the beck. This paved path leads to a modern suburban street. Turn right and keep going until you reach a T-junction.

GRADE: 2
ESTIMATED CALORIE BURN: 420

Distance: 4 miles
Time: 2 hours
Terrain: Mostly flat along roads, grass and forest tracks.
Number of stiles: 0
Starting point: Outside St Mary's church, Broughton. GR 961086.
How to get there: Take the A18 east from Scunthorpe. Turn left along the B1207 leading to Broughton. When you reach the T-junction turn left and park on the road near to the church. Hourly buses from Scunthorpe go through Broughton from Monday to Saturday.
OS map: Landranger 112 Scunthorpe & Gainsborough.
Refreshments: You pass several shops and two pubs – the Red Lion (tel. 01652 652560) and the Thatch Inn (01652 655565) – in Broughton town near the start and near the end of the walk.

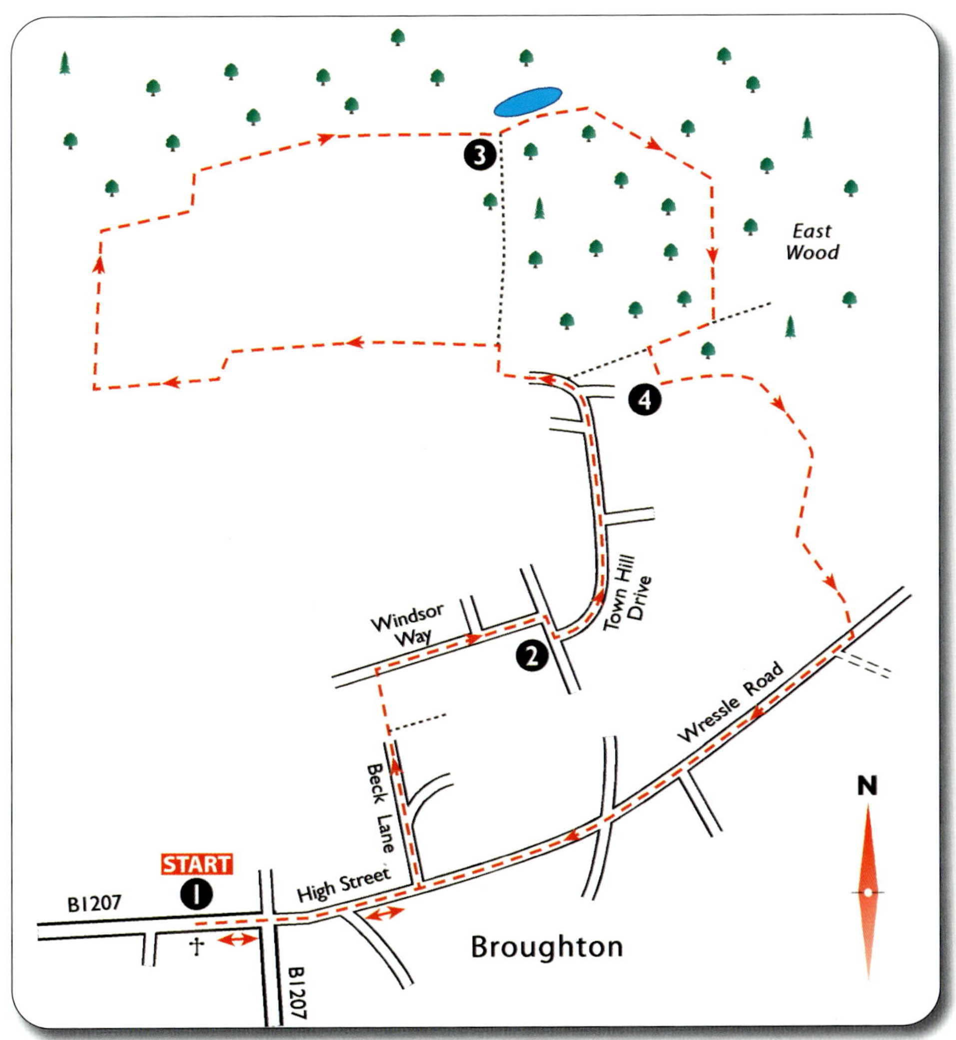

2 At the T-junction turn right, then immediately left up **Town Hill Drive**. This takes you gradually uphill, curving left through suburban houses. At the top ignore the first footpath sign right but take the next one which runs parallel to a track with conifers on your left-hand side. Follow the conifers for around 50 yards, where a footpath sign points you right. Take this path for around 20 yards but when you reach a gate ignore the public footpath sign straight on and instead turn left to follow the **Countryside Commission** (Natural England) walk. Suddenly you're in lovely open grass fields with woodland

■ *On the route back to Broughton* ■

behind and to your right, houses behind a hedge to the left and a series of broken hedges ahead of you. Dog walkers love this area because there is so much open space.

Stay to the left of the field and continue until you reach the third broken hedge straight ahead. Follow the hedge that has been running parallel to you round to the left and back to the right again. Continue to follow it until you reach the fourth broken hedge. Here turn 90° to the right so that the broken hedge is now on your left. Walk towards the deciduous trees and on a clear day you may catch a glimpse of the **Wolds** in the far right corner above the tree tops. When you reach the trees, turn right and follow the line of the woodland by taking a left down the slope and back round to the right. The trees to your left are reasonably sparse with a stream running parallel to you and a slope up the other side. After around 100 yards you reach a broken hedge after which the path veers slightly to the right, taking you away from the trees on your left and through a gap in the next broken hedge.

3 Now aim for the trees straight in front of you in the left corner of the field. When you reach them, duck through a small gap in the hedge and follow the well maintained path diagonally left. The wood is a beautiful mix of pine and deciduous trees. Soon you will see a pond and a farmhouse to your left between the trees. Cross a stream and you have reached a good spot for a picnic. There are no seats here but if it's dry the bank of the pond is a nice place to sit and absorb the tranquillity. At the footpath junction take a right where the sign points to **Brigg Road**. A little wooden bridge crosses a stream and a narrower path takes you through smaller trees. After a few yards take the left fork and after a few more yards ignore the path passing left to right. When the path reaches a group of conifers take a sharp right, following the footpath sign. There is the odd muddy patch along here but slipping on fallen pine cones is perhaps more of a risk! At the T-junction of paths turn right and after a few yards turn left.

4 You soon leave the woods and turn immediately left, so the trees are now to your left-hand side and you have a lovely view over the fields with woodland in the distance to your right. After walking through a gap in the hedge, follow the path which forks to the right and winds its way down the slope through the grass field, leading to the gate in front of the road. When you reach the road turn right and walk along the pavement. After around 200 yards you reach **Broughton** again, where you continue along **High Street**. There are a couple of benches here should you need a rest and the **Thatch Inn** to your left serves hot food. Continue past the chapel you saw earlier and past the **Red Lion pub** back to the church.

Stamford to Easton-on-the-Hill

A Beautiful Circuit

■ *Stamford seen from The Meadows* ■

What a **wonderful** place **Stamford** is. The town has a wealth of history with its cobbled streets, eleven churches and the impressive **Burghley House** on its doorstep. Visitors flock here by the day and many movie makers have chosen to film here, including the creators of

Pride and Prejudice. Over the years **Stamford** has been a town known for its pottery and wool. It could also have developed into a famous university town had King Edward III not banned disgruntled Oxford students and tutors from studying in Stamford in the 14th century, after they preferred the town ahead of the poor conditions in their colleges. This walk starts at another great attraction – **Stamford Meadows** – which is packed in the summer months with people playing sports, eating ice cream and relaxing in the sun. The route takes you up to **Easton-on-the-Hill**, where there are frequently great views back to the town. It then takes you to **Wothorpe House** before heading back to **Stamford** once more.

1 From **Bath Row**, cross the bridge over a stream into the park and head diagonally right towards the river. When you reach it, turn right and follow the river until you reach a fence. Look back here for a fabulous view of the park with the town and its many spires behind. Walk through the wooden gate and continue along the middle of the three paths ahead. You're now in a much wilder field – a gorgeous meadow with long green grass and wild flowers in summer. Continue through the meadow along the same path, aiming for the bridge crossing the river ahead. When you reach the bridge, cross it and turn right again so the river is running parallel on your right. After around 150 yards, when the path forks, take the left fork so that you're now heading away from the river towards a tunnel under the road

GRADE: 2
ESTIMATED CALORIE BURN: 520

Distance: 5½ miles
Time: 2½ hours
Terrain: There are two hills to climb during this walk. Most of the walk is along grass fields and tracks.
Number of stiles: 9
Starting point: Bath Row, Stamford. GR 037069.
How to get there: From the A1 south turn left along the A606 into Stamford. Continue along Scotgate, turn right along All Saints Street, second left along Sheep Market, right along Castle Dyke and left along Bath Row, where you can park. Regular buses run from Peterborough, as well as hourly trains.
OS map: Landranger 141 Kettering & Corby.
Refreshments: Stamford has plenty of restaurants, cafés and pubs. The Blue Bell pub at Easton-on-the-Hill serves food (tel. 01780 763003).

(such is the beauty of this area that even the cars seem to hush a little while driving past). Cross the first stile leading through the tunnel. Then cross a stream at the other side and continue across a field, aiming for the wooden bridge leading to the railway line.

2 Cross the railway line and walk down the steps on the other side. A boardwalk guides you over a swampy area and a path leads you through a field and up a slight slope to the trees on the other side. When you reach the trees the path becomes a track leading through the wood, up the hill. As you continue past the wood the land drops down into a valley to your left. When you reach the end of the field take a breather to look back at **Stamford** rising up over the trees.

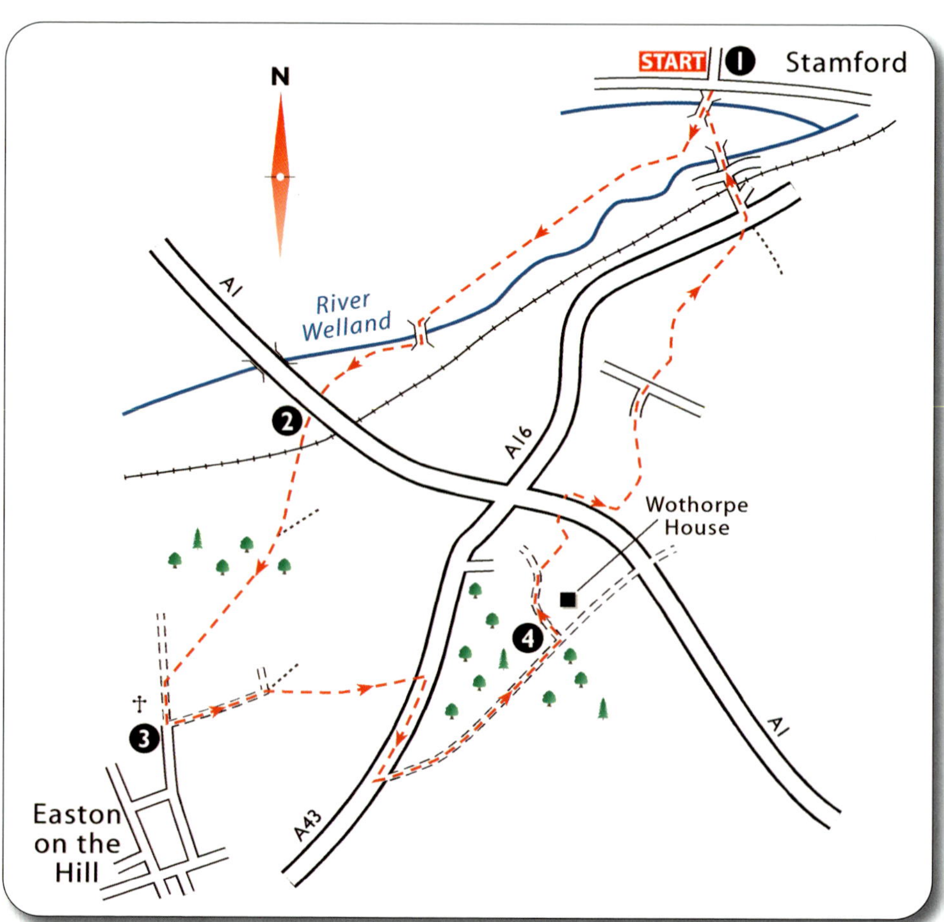

Then, instead of following the track left, cut through the gap in the hedge and walk through the next field aiming for the large house ahead. Continue in the same direction, crossing a couple more stiles, then cross the wide driveway to the road straight ahead. Turn left along the road, which isn't even paved at first, and pass **All Saints' church**, parts of which date back to the 12th century. There is a footpath left here along **Park Walk** just beyond **Courtyard House**. But I would recommend first having a wander around **Easton-on-the-Hill** with its fantastic old houses and pristine little cottages. The short route I would suggest is first right up **The Lane**, left up **West Street**, left along **High Street** (past the **Blue Bell pub**, which serves hot food) and left again at the memorial down **Church Street**.

3 This brings you back to that footpath along **Park Walk**, which heads along a track, slightly downhill. Follow the brick wall on your left. At the end don't follow the track to the left, or the footpath straight ahead. Instead take the footpath in a one o'clock direction. This path is often unclear. Cross the stream over a little bridge at the bottom and cross the stile. Aim for the far left corner of the next field if the path is unclear, over the stile, and if the path is still unclear cut through the field up the hill aiming for the large gap in the hedge in front of the main road. When you reach the road turn right and follow the road for around 200 yards. Then take a sharp left along a bridleway with a hedge to the left and fence to the right. This leads you through a beautiful wood where you may be able to spot deer if you're lucky. Follow the path right through the wood, where it opens out with fields to your left and the grand ruin of **Wothorpe House** in front of you.

4 At the bridleway junction, take the left turn between the new trees with Wothorpe House to your right and old woodland to your left. Cross the dirt track and continue along the grass track between the new trees parallel to the stony track. When you reach the end take the stile over the fence to join the footpath through the field past the lovely cottage to your right. Aim to the right of a small copse with a pond in the middle, then follow the track straight on, just to the right of an old store barn. When you reach the other side of the barn follow the green arrow left with the fence now on your right as you head straight for the A1. The stream is now to your left and the path heads through a kissing gate before continuing under the tunnel. When on the other side, turn right along the edge of the field, with the road to your right. At the end of the field turn left and continue, with the wall running on your left-hand side. Keep to the left of the field, curving left and at the end cross the stile and head diagonally left to the far corner of the field. Cross the next stile, cross the tiny bridges and then take the

■ *Wothorpe House, passed on the route* ■

gravel path between two lovely thick hedges with beautiful gardens either side.

The path joins a road, which you follow until you reach a T-junction. Look for the yellow footpath arrow straight ahead (next to the grand house on the right) and another narrow path leads between two more hedges. It curves left, across a bridge, through the gate, then diagonally left through a grass field to the far left corner with **Stamford** straight in front of you. Cross the track, the bridge and then the stile before following the clear cut path towards the next hedge. Walk through the gate and follow the fence on your right which leads through a hedge to the road. Cross the road and walk along **Wothorpe Road**, following it round to the left, past the beautiful old buildings and over the railway line. Don't follow the road round to the right, but continue straight over the car park, over a footbridge and straight back through the park.

 12 Skegness to Winthorpe
A Seaside Stride

■ *The famous Skegness beach* ■

Why not enjoy one of Lincolnshire's main attractions while continuing your series of fitness walks? **Skegness** and its beautiful beach attract thousands of visitors each year. Immortalised by its famous mascot – the Jolly Fisherman – the town was the site of the first Butlin's holiday resort in 1936. In summer the town really comes to life with its 125-year-old pier and abundance of live shows, fairground rides, slot machines, bars and donkey rides. This walk takes you an unusual and surprisingly tranquil way to the beach via a long stretch of woodland, farm fields and the village of **Winthorpe**. You then walk along the beach back towards **Skegness**. The real hustle and bustle will be towards the end of the walk. If you would rather avoid this, try walking early in the morning or outside of school holidays.

1 Follow the footpath sign opposite the yellow **Skegness Sports Centre** sign and to the left of **Elizabeth Grove**. A paved path takes you between two wooden fences and you're almost immediately out of the town. After a quick left-right, walk through the lovely avenue of trees with the caravan

GRADE: 2
ESTIMATED CALORIE BURN: 500

Distance: 5½ miles
Time: 2½ hours
Terrain: No hills, mostly grass tracks in the early stages, then sandy underfoot towards the end.
Number of stiles: 1
Starting point: Outside the football ground at Skegness. GR 562642.
How to get there: Enter Skegness along the A158. Park on the roadside next to the football ground, which is on your right-hand side. There are buses to Skegness every hour from Lincoln and Boston, with an infrequent service from Lincoln on Sunday. Trains from Boston and Sleaford arrive at least every 2 hours from Monday to Saturday.
OS map: Landranger 122 Skegness & Horncastle.
Refreshments: There is the Charnwood Tavern (tel. 01754 764725) a third of the way along and an abundance of restaurants, cafés, shops and pubs in Skegness at the end, or perhaps you might enjoy a picnic on the beach.

park to your right. The path winds through the trees with grass either side of it. The long thin park is popular with dog walkers and there are many benches along the way. The path soon becomes unpaved and gets gradually thinner. Eventually the caravan park to your right makes way for houses. If you lose the path here keep to the right. At the end you see a wooden footbridge to the right and a deep dyke straight in front of you with a field behind it. Ignore the bridge and turn left, following the grass path with the dyke to your right and the trees to the left. The faint path follows the dyke, crossing several smaller dykes, until you eventually leave the woods. The final bench here is the last one for a while so now would be a good time to stop for a breather if needed. Turn right, crossing the dyke, and follow the path through the field towards the houses opposite. When you reach the lane follow it right and take the first lane left, marked with a 'dead end' sign.

2 The road curves right, then left again. Ahead to your left you can see the lovely **St Mary's church**. Just before reaching the white **Charnwood Tavern** on your right a signposted footpath takes you right up a driveway. Ahead of you is a large roller-coaster rising from the horizon. Just before you reach a stile turn right, climbing another stile, and continue straight on, following the dyke to your right. The dyke bends to the left and back round to the right before straightening and heading towards red-brick houses. The grassy track may be unclear and overgrown at times but so long as the dyke is always on your right-hand side you won't go wrong. Eventually you meet a fence with a ditch behind it just before reaching the houses. Turn left, then turn right across the wooden bridge. Turn right again, so there is a hedge to your left and a fence and the dyke to your right. When you reach the street aim slightly to the left, towards the 'Strictly No Ball Games' sign, and continue down that street.

3 Cross **Count Alan Road** and continue along **Spirewic Avenue** as it winds its way to the main road. Use the pedestrian crossing to go over the road here and turn left along the paved footpath. Take the first street right, **North Foreland Drive**, which is marked with a footpath sign. The road soon

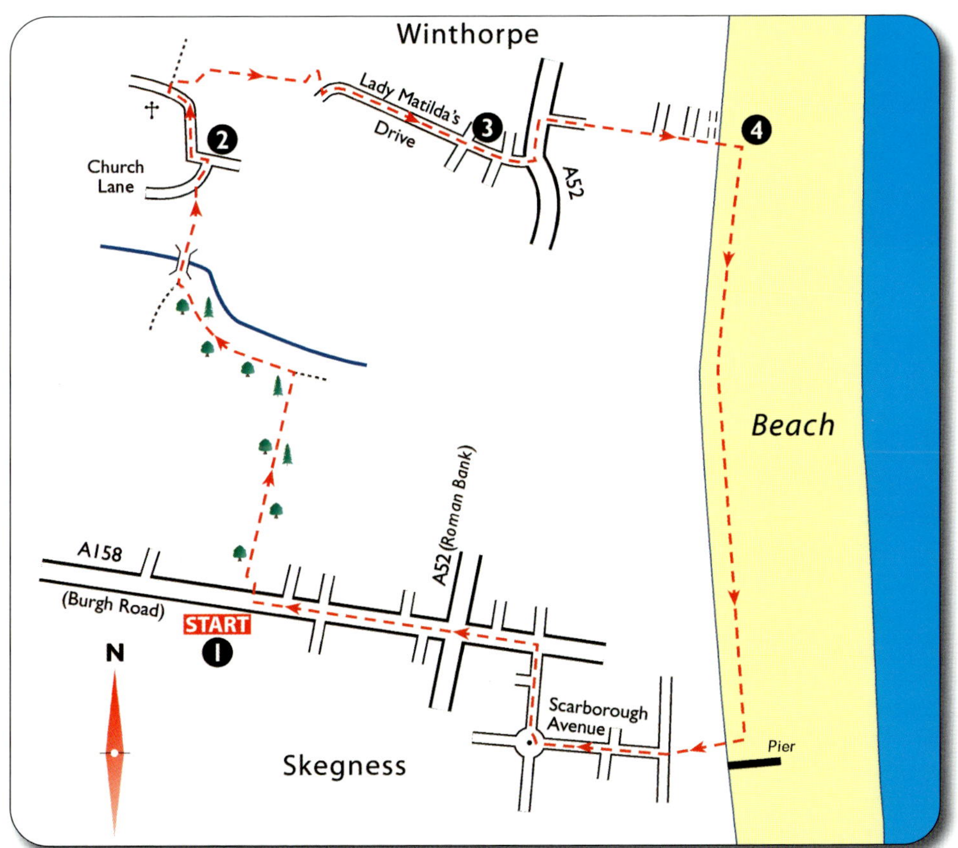

comes to a dead end but a paved path continues straight on. Follow it and you will soon see a golf course to your right. The path leads up a slight slope, where at the top you can see the glistening **North Sea** straight ahead for the first time in the walk. When you reach it you are greeted by a lovely sandy beach extending for miles either side, with a promenade to your left and **Skegness pier** in the far distance to your right. There is also a wind farm out to sea in front of you. If you have brought a picnic with you for this walk, it really is 'take your pick' for your perfect spot along the beach.

■ *Near the start of the walk* ■

4 Turn right, taking the steps down to the sand and continue along the shoreline. Soon you will see the sea defence rocks appear in the sand dunes to your right. This section is popular with dog walkers and fishermen. Continue towards the pier, with fairground rides also in view behind it. If the sand is too much underfoot a concrete promenade called **Seaview Walk** (later becoming **Prince Edward Walk**) begins on your right and may be a better option. This also gives a beautiful and slightly elevated view of the coastline. Just before reaching the pier, take the path diagonally right and turn right again across a concrete bridge over a small river. Continue along the path with the park to your right and bowling alley to the left. When you reach the main road you find yourself in the heart of glitzy **Skegness** with its souvenir shops, bingo halls, amusement arcades, pubs, cafés and hotels. A block away to your left is the town's clock tower and there are benches here should you need a break. Cross the road and continue down **Scarborough Avenue**, along which are plenty of hotels and bed and breakfasts. It is also very quiet compared to the busy seafront. At the large roundabout with the church in the middle, turn right down the leafy **Lumley Avenue**. At the end turn left, walk to the traffic lights, cross the main road and continue up **Burgh Road** which leads you back to the beginning.

13 Blyton to Laughton

A Test of Stamina

FOOTPATHS FOR FITNESS

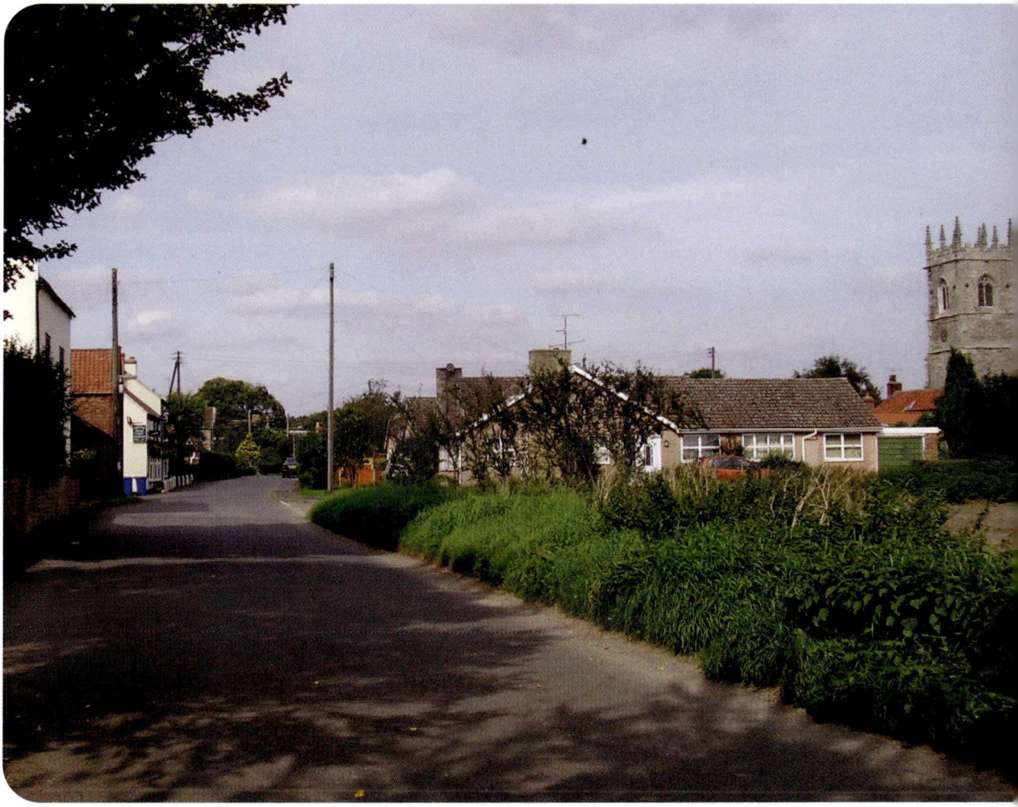

■ *Laughton village* ■

For some time the locals in this area have been fighting tirelessly against a wind farm being built in the region. And when you wander through you can see why the prospect angers them so much. The landscape is either open farmland or an abundance of forest with the odd ancient pond or rare heath land scattered around. The walk begins at **Blyton** – a village set on the busy A159. It's only a small place but has an overwhelming number of services for its size including a café, Chinese takeaway, local shop, two pubs (including the 250-year-old Black Horse Inn) and even a very popular ice cream parlour! The route then takes you through the woods to the quiet village of **Laughton**, near which there have been numerous prehistoric finds. There are some hills along the way, but obvious stopping points are few and far between so this walk should be a good test of stamina and, if speed is your thing, a good chance to work up some pace.

1 Follow the small lane away from the village with the football pitches to your right. There will soon be a row of trees to the left that produce beautiful white flowers at various times of the year. This sweet little country lane soon turns left and dips down a small hill. There are green hedges either side of you and **Laughton church** is visible in the distance to your right. After 150 more yards turn left to cross a wooden bridge over the dyke. Turn right again and follow the track with the dyke to your right-hand side. Another track will join the one you're walking on, running side by side, and there are farm fields either side of you. After around 300 yards the track bends to the left, still following the dyke on your right-hand side. The path here is a mixture of mud and grass. It's a good time to build up speed if you wish and you're heading straight for the woods which are a treasure in this region. Apart from the odd tree scattered here and there, the first signs of woodland you reach are giant conifer trees on the right-hand side, behind the dyke. These continue for around 400 yards after which you have trees either side of you.

GRADE: 2
ESTIMATED CALORIE BURN: 500

Distance: 5½ miles
Time: 2½ hours
Terrain: A few slopes, mostly tracks and roads. Towards the end you walk over fields that can be muddy after wet weather.
Number of stiles: 0
Starting point: Sandbeck Lane, Blyton. GR 849948.
How to get there: From Gainsborough take the A159 north to Blyton. When you reach the village turn left up Sandbeck Lane and park at the side of the road. Buses from Gainsborough and Scunthorpe run once an hour from Monday to Saturday.
OS map: Landranger 112 Scunthorpe & Gainsborough.
Refreshments: Blyton has a café, shop and two pubs serving meals, the White Hart (tel. 01427 628683) and the Black Horse Inn (tel. 01427 628277). Laughton, two-thirds of the way along the walk, also has a pub serving food, the Ingram Arms (tel. 01427 628465).

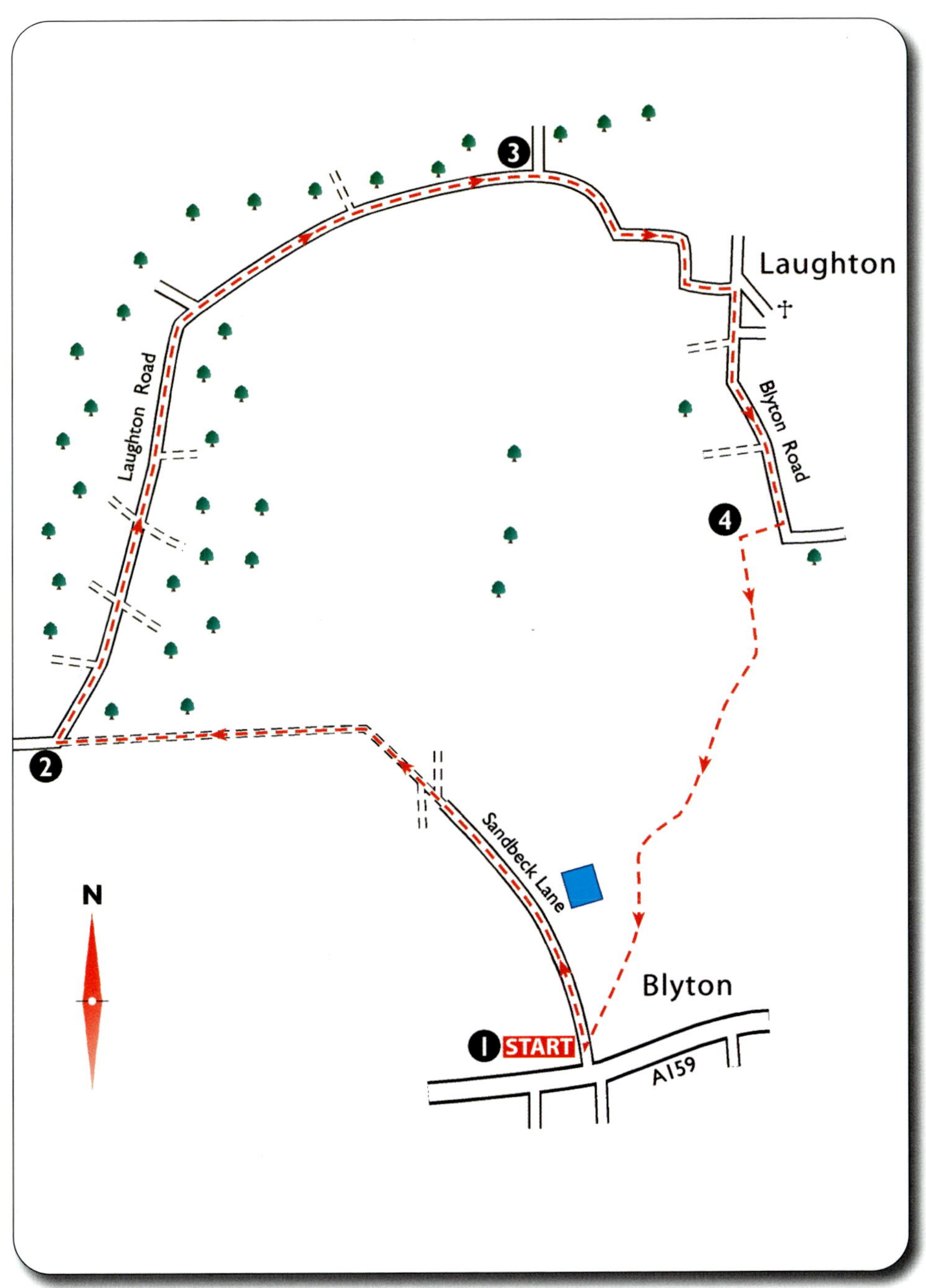

Laughton
Laughton Road
Blyton Road
Sandbeck Lane
Blyton
START
A159
N

■ *On the way to the woods* ■

2 Eventually you reach a car park. Walk through this, until you come to the road, where you turn right. The road continues straight for a while, with woodland to the right and soon a giant farm field to the left. Continue past the track left leading to the delightfully-named **Warp Farm** and **Whoofer Farm**. You now have woodland on both sides. The road is not a busy one and when there are no cars around is very tranquil with just the sound of the wind in the trees and bird song to keep you company. After another 300 yards pass a footpath and red-brick houses to your left. After a while the road bends to the right. Ignore the turning left to **Wildsworth** but admire the beautiful semi-detached cottages to your left soon after this that make you feel envious of those who live there. The woodland soon clears to the right, giving you glimpses of **Laughton** as you go. After crossing a stream the road takes you through the last section of pine wood for the walk. The lane bends to the right again before joining another road on a corner. Continue straight on along **Morton Road** and into **Laughton** village.

3 This peaceful village has some very pretty houses on show as you follow the winding street to reach a crossroads. Turn right here and you will soon pass the attractive timber-framed **Ingram Arms**, which serves hot food, should you need a bite. The road continues out of the village again and up a slight slope. This has a bench at the top which is a perfect picnic spot with a fine view across the landscape. From here you can see a small copse in the foreground, the larger woodland behind it and even the top of a power station at ten o'clock. **Blyton** is on the hill to your left with its prominent church and windmill. To your right you can also see Laughton church spire. Continue along the road and, after 400 yards, when the road turns left, take instead the track leading right.

4 Follow it as it bends left so that there is a small wood approximately 200 yards on your left. When you reach a small pond surrounded by trees to the right, follow the yellow arrow leading you along a path between a hedge and some trees, ignoring the track swinging to the right. Continue through another field until the footpath bends diagonally right (at the third telegraph pole you reach in the field itself). At the end of that field, cross a small wooden bridge over a stream and continue in the same direction across the next field, which is now leading slightly uphill.

At the end of the field turn diagonally right and continue, following a hedge to your left. You will soon reach a gap in the hedge in front of you. Make sure you ignore the path 90° to your left and instead take the path 45° to your left. Follow the path through the field as it gradually winds round to the right. Just before reaching the hedge with the reservoir behind, you meet a junction of paths. Turn left, following a hedge to your right. When the hedge stops continue along the same path through the long grass and then cut straight across the football fields (provided there is no game on) aiming for the far right corner. Walk through the gate on the right-hand side of the footpath sign and turn left along the lane, taking you back to the start.

14 Tealby to Walesby
Take up the Challenge

■ *Heading for Walesby* ■

Versions of this walk are popular among ramblers because it takes you through two beautiful villages, provides stunning views over the west of the county, and its steep climbs and descents make it a challenge for any trekker. Tealby boasts one of the oldest pubs in Britain, the King's Head, with its handsome thatched roof. The village was also home to the poet Sir Alfred Lord Tennyson's parents and, more recently, Elton John's lyricist, Bernie Taupin. Walesby, meanwhile, has the lonely All Saint's church standing on a hill above the village. It had been the parish church until 1914 and was on the verge of collapse until thankfully it was saved

GRADE: 2
ESTIMATED CALORIE BURN: 600

Distance: 6 miles
Time: 3 hours
Terrain: Often steep climbs and descents along mostly tracks and grass paths. Sections can be boggy after wet weather.
Number of stiles: 5
Starting point: Front Street, Tealby. GR 156906
How to get there: Take the B1203 east of Market Rasen towards Tealby, turn right down Cow Lane, then left onto Sandy Lane and left onto Front Street where there is roadside parking available.
OS map: Landranger 113 Grimsby, Louth & Market Rasen.
Refreshments: The Kings Head (tel. 01673 838347) at the start of the route, plus a village shop and a tea room. Walesby also has a tea room.

and still stands proud today. I believe this walk is as tough as any in this book because of the steep climbs and boggy patches throughout the journey. But if you can accomplish this, you are certainly ready to tackle the longer Grade 3 walks with confidence.

1. Walk up the hill, away from the **Kings Head** pub, and just before reaching the hedge, take the footpath left, signed to **Rasen Road**. Follow the grass field uphill on the right and a gate in the far right corner takes you between houses, down a drive and to the main road. Cross the road, turn right and walk along the pavement for a few yards before taking the footpath left up a driveway. Once you walk through the gate you'll find yourself in open sheep fields with the hill rising to your right and the first impressive views to your left. The mown grass path undulates before dropping to a kissing gate in the far left-hand corner of the field. Continue straight ahead. At the footpath junction take the boardwalk bridge right along the **Viking Way**, ignoring the bridge on your left, and continue along the boggy ground. Walk alongside the fence on the left, through the gateway and follow the path up the hill. At the sign, cut through the little valley aiming to the left of the group of trees at the top. This is the first tough climb of the day but it's worth it because a quick glance behind gives good views over **Tealby** and the edge of the **Wolds**. When you reach the farm, with the unusual looking farmhouse, turn right into the wood so the hedge is on your left and the trees on your right. A gate takes you out of the wood. Follow the path

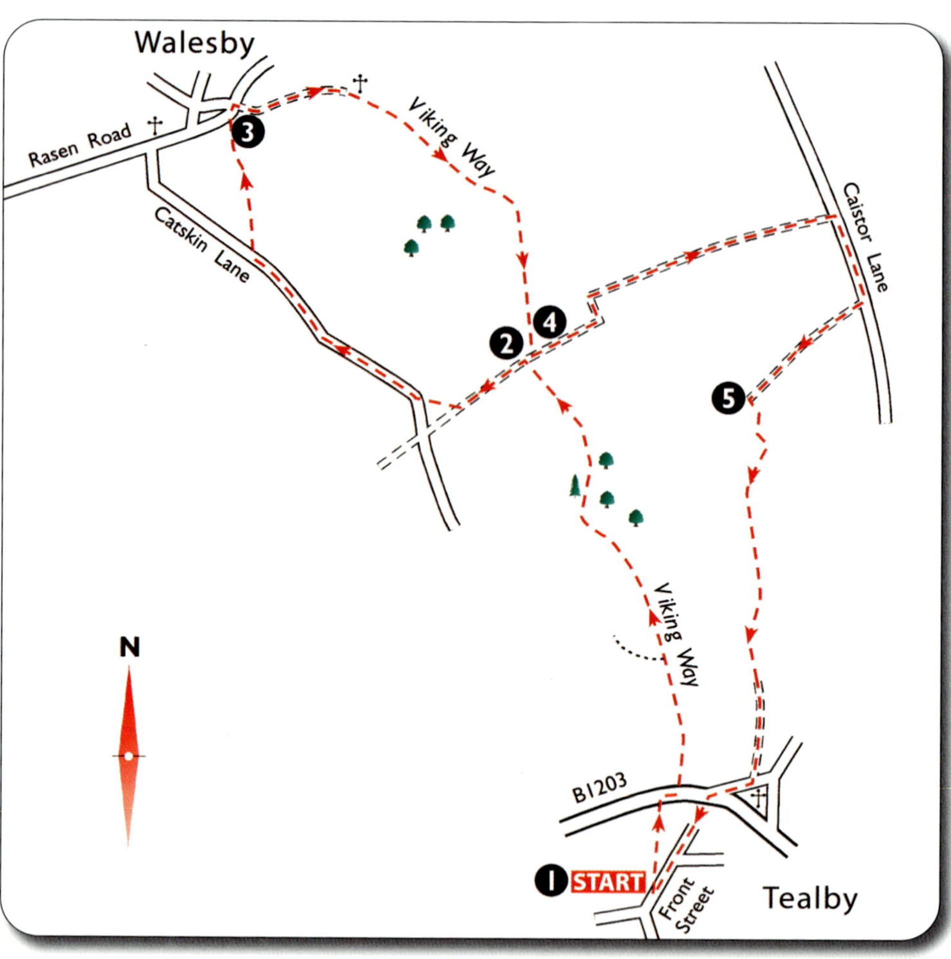

diagonally left down the hill and around the pond to the far left corner of the field. Turn 45° to the right and follow the fence to the paved farm track.

2 Turn left to walk downhill towards the road at the bottom. Just before reaching the road, turn right over a stile and go straight across the field to another stile which drops you on the road. Next to this stile is the first bench you reach, though it looks a tad uncomfortable to say the least. Turn right along **Catskin Lane**, a narrow road with tall hedges to either side. Ignore the green-arrowed footpath to your right and take the yellow-arrowed path right a little further on, just before a big red-brick house. This takes you diagonally left through a boggy heath field and gradually uphill. Eventually the path reaches a wooden bridge – cross that and turn left along the muddy path, then right alongside a garden with a wooden fence on your right. A narrow gap in the wall leads you to the road and you have reached the quaint village of **Walesby**.

If you need a break here, there is a tea shop down the road to your left and there are benches in **St Mary's churchyard** – the church itself was damaged in the earthquake of 2008. But I would recommend going on to

■ *Front Street, Tealby* ■

All Saints church if you have brought your own picnic. To do this, turn right and on the road corner walk up the track, continuing straight on when a track bends round to the right after about 20 yards. What follows is a steep and tiring climb to the top of the dirt track. A bench sits three quarters the way up if you fancy a breather and at the top, all on its own, stands the beautiful **All Saints church** – parts of which date back to the 12th century. The building can still be used as a church, though the floor and benches look very bare. The beautiful stained-glass windows are worth a look, and you can't fail to spot the best views of the walk from the church's elevated position. After walking through the gate at the other side of the churchyard, walk diagonally left along the left of the field, then through arable fields, aiming left of the wood ahead. After you pass through the deer fence, fork left again through the bushes to the bottom of the valley. Then you have the inevitable task of climbing up the other side. It's very steep, but once at the top the path gradually descends to the paved farm track you walked along earlier.

4 When you reach it turn left and walk past the drive on your left before taking a quick left-right through the farmyard. The track continues uphill – the last uphill section of the walk. Continue all the way to the road, turn right and then take the first right down a farm track. This section is a great opportunity to gather pace. Once in the farmyard turn 90° left and walk to the gate. Go through the gate, turn right for a few yards then left along the path to the gate the other side. It's worth taking a glance back here to the charmingly crumbly looking farmhouse.

5 Cut through the next field and continue straight on over three stiles. After the third stile the path bends to the right, where you aim just left of the tree ahead before turning back round to the left, aiming to the right of the houses.

Follow the track straight downhill, turning right at the church. Cross the main road and continue straight towards the bench. After the bench, turn left and a footpath takes you downhill to a quiet street that looks straight from the 1950s. When you reach the butcher's shop continue straight on to finish this tough challenge.

15 Norton Disney

Walt was here!

FOOTPATHS FOR FITNESS

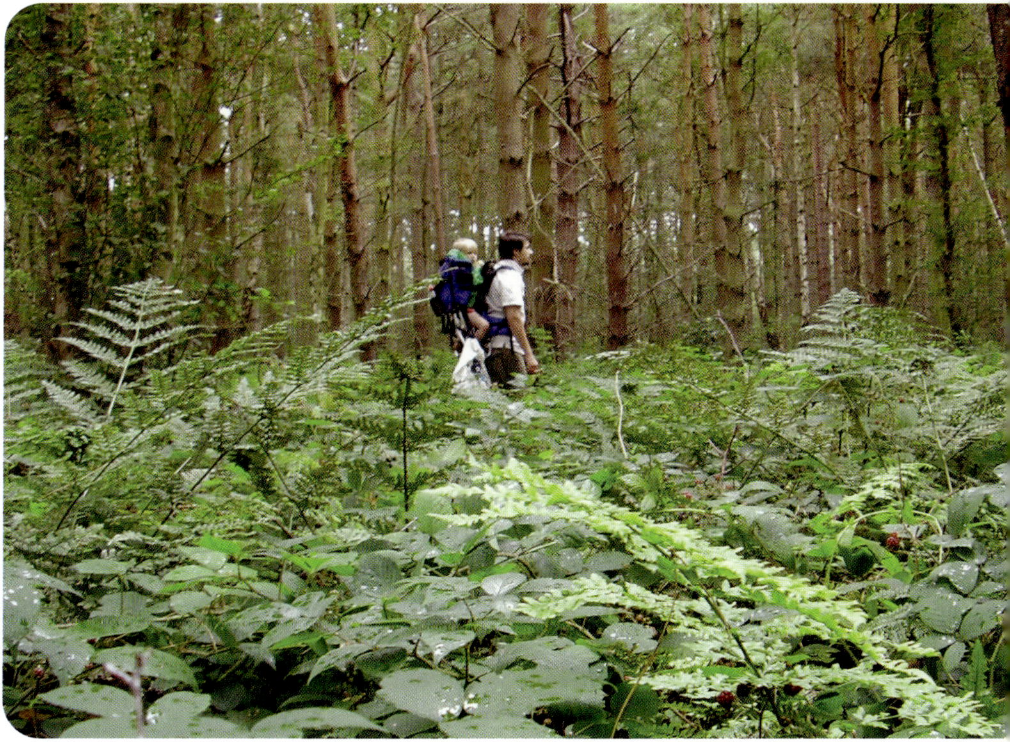

In the woods near Stapleford

Set in the picturesque Witham valley, this walk takes you through two quiet villages and along the edge of **Stapleford Woods**, situated on the border of Nottinghamshire and Lincolnshire. **Norton Disney**, named after the D'Isigny family who settled here after the Norman invasion in 1066, was once visited by Walt Disney in an attempt to trace his ancestors. The walk begins opposite the **St Vincent Arms**, named after the famous naval battle of Cape St Vincent in 1797. The village commemorated the battle a century later by planting 100 horse chestnut trees between the church and the village hall, many of which still stand today. The walk has no difficult climbs but there are few places to sit along the way, making it a good test of endurance and a sign that you're ready for longer walks.

1 Leave the car park and turn right. Continue out of the village so you are walking along a narrow road with trees to either side. You soon pass a small cluster of houses and a large barn, after which there are hedges to either side with fields behind. **Norton Big Wood** is situated in the distance to your right. Pass another group of red-brick houses before continuing past **Norton Lodge Centre** and hotel to your left. You quickly return to a canopy of trees on either side and begin to climb a gradual slope. Look for the bridleway sign to your left and take the track towards the woods.

2 The track has fields on either side and, after 300 yards, a bank with gorse bushes runs parallel to your right-hand side. Pass the cabins and cross over the conveyor belt running under the track carrying materials from the quarry. A huge crater with boggy patches at the base greets you to the right-hand side and the track takes you straight to the woods, passing small ponds both left and right. Enter the woods via a bridge over a stream, ignore the path straight on and take the one diagonally right. The path takes you firstly through deciduous trees, then through pine trees. Go straight across one major track, following the blue arrows. When you reach the second major track, cross it and continue straight ahead, ignoring the blue arrows leading left. A little further on, the wood opens out a little and you pass a field to your left. Continue through the sturdy and more open woodland until you reach the road. Turn left here and turn right at the T-junction. Follow the road with thick hedges reaching right to its edge, as it takes you past a farm

GRADE: 2
ESTIMATED CALORIE BURN: 580

Distance: 6 miles
Time: 3 hours
Terrain: No real hills, either road, dirt tracks or arable fields underfoot.
Number of stiles: 0
Starting point: Norton Disney village hall car park. GR 887592.
How to get there: From the Lincoln bypass take the A46 towards Newark. At the first roundabout turn left into Witham St Hughs. Drive through the village, turn right at the T-junction, then left along Swinderby Road into Norton Disney. Turn left at the T-junction and park in the village hall car park opposite the pub.
OS map: Landranger 121 Lincoln & Newark-on-Trent.
Refreshments: There is a pub in Norton Disney, the St Vincent Arms, which serves food (tel. 01522 789987).

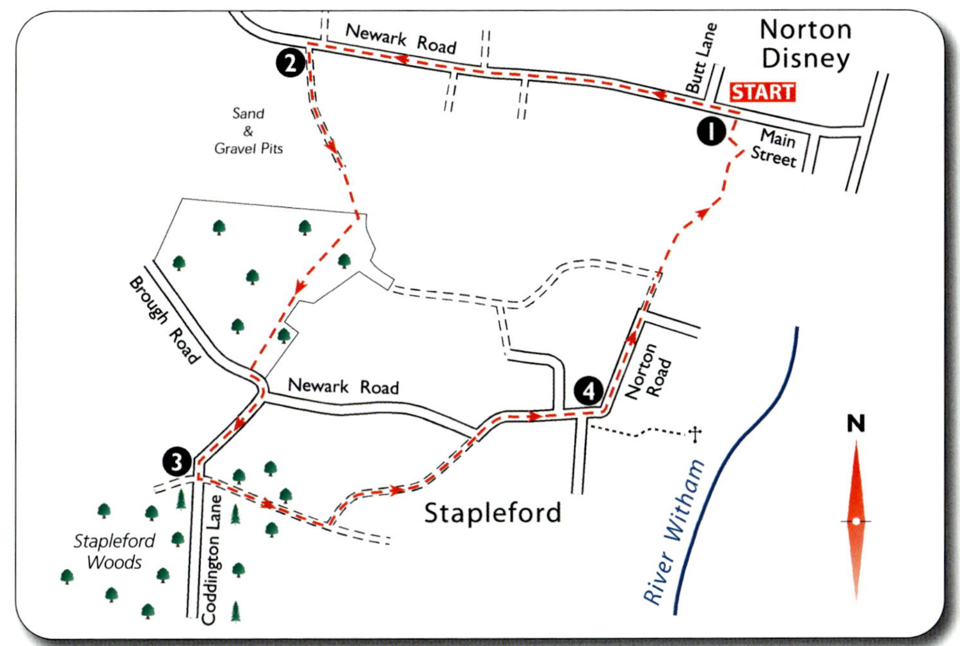

on your right-hand side and into **Stapleford Woods**. When you turn the corner, look for the sign welcoming you to the woods and turn left along the paved lane through the woods.

3 This straight lane takes you through to the other side of the wood and continues with fields either side. Before reaching the red-brick house, turn left along the footpath which winds through a field. It is common to hear rifle shots around here but don't worry – you're well out of range! The path veers slightly to the right, passing the occasional tree, many of which are either dead or dying and can look impressively gnarled. The track slowly curves back to the left before joining the road. Continue straight on to enter the tiny village of **Stapleford**. The road curves right and a pavement starts on your left after around 100 yards, which you can follow through the village. The route takes you left, following **Norton Road** out of the village. But if you fancy a picnic the village church and neighbouring **River Witham** is a nice place to stop. To get there, turn right down **Beckingham Road** just before the road through the village curves to the left. After a few paces a footpath leads left straight to the sweet little church. When you have finished come back the way you came and rejoin the route heading out of the village.

■ *All Saints church, Stapleford* ■

4 After leaving the village the road bends right. Ignore this bend and instead take the track straight on. You are now surrounded by fields again, with the cliff in the distance to your right and **Norton Disney** in front of you. When you reach the end of the first field on your left, leave the track so that you're walking in the same direction as before, with the hedge now on your left. A yellow footpath arrow guides you in the right direction. Follow the path for a while, and shortly before reaching a lone dying tree, a post points you diagonally right. Follow it through the field – the path is often very unclear here, in which case aim directly for the church. When you reach the end of the field cross the wooden bridge and continue along the left of the next field with several bushes to your left. When you reach the tree, continue straight through the field towards the kissing gate the other side. The gate leads you to a narrow path between a hedge and small trees. Follow the path when it takes a sharp left, keep to the right of the field, then follow it back round to the right. This takes you firstly across a section of grass, then through a pub car park and to the road, where the village hall car park is straight in front of you.

16 Little Bytham and Castle Bytham

A Viaduct Runs Through

■ *On the way back to Little Bytham* ■

This walk is set in rolling countryside that easily compares to the beauty of the Wolds. It also takes you through two very picturesque villages, both of which have their own unique charm. **Little Bytham**, where the walk begins, has a great village shop which could be from another age. The old-fashioned fuel pumps outside add to the feeling of a 1950s' rural experience. The most obvious feature in the village, though, is the huge viaduct that cuts straight through the middle. Every few minutes you can hear the whistle of a passing train along the top of the construction. **Castle Bytham** is larger but no less charming, with rows of sweet cottages, good pubs and stunning gardens. The main feature of this village is the large grass mound where a Saxon castle once stood. Built in the 11th century, it was destroyed by Henry III in the 13th century, when he was just fourteen. The village has been a conservation area since 1973. This walk is very enjoyable and is also a good test which should develop your fitness and ability to manage small hills.

GRADE: 2
ESTIMATED CALORIE BURN: 600

Distance: 6 miles
Time: 3 hours
Terrain: There are several small hills. Part of the walk is along roads and part across farm fields.
Number of stiles: 4
Starting point: Opposite New Estate, Little Bytham. GR 012180.
How to get there: From the centre of Bourne take the A151 west. Turn left along the A6121 before turning right towards Witham on the Hill. Continue straight through the village until you reach a T-junction. Turn right into Little Bytham, turn left at the T-junction in the village and park opposite New Estate on the edge of the village. A few buses travel to Little Bytham from Grantham and Stamford from Monday to Saturday.
OS map: Landranger 130 Grantham, Sleaford & Bourne.
Refreshments: Little Bytham has one village shop. Castle Bytham has two pubs – the Fox and Hounds (tel. 01780 410336) and the Castle (tel. 01780 410504) – both serving food, and a shop.

1 Continue along the road heading away from the village. After passing new houses on the left you soon have farm fields to your left and right. Walk quickly past the sewage works to your left and under the electricity pylons before following a stream running parallel on the left-hand side. You're now at the bottom of a valley and, after a short while, the stream swings away to the left. Look for the footpath sign behind the beige brick and cream coloured house on your right. Follow the track and continue straight ahead when the first track swings to the left. After around 100 yards, turn left just before reaching the gate, so the field is on your left and the hedge on the right. Behind the hedge is what looks like an old quarry, but is now a green area of small trees and bushes. Cross the stile and walk to the left-hand side of the bushes running through the middle. When you reach a large gap in the bushes, walk diagonally right to the right of another set of bushes in front of you. There is a great view across the small valley into **Castle Bytham** to your left. Walk through the gap in the bushes and head downhill along the track towards the turquoise wooden hut.

2 Pass the hut and continue downhill, over the next stile and straight down the lane alongside the very shallow stream. Cross the stream and look for the very old stone bench on your right. Also to your right is the large mound which was the site of the Saxon castle. Sadly the land is private, but for an excellent view turn right at the T-junction and sit on the bench either next to the pond or on another bench 20 yards further, surrounded by beautiful grey stone buildings with pristine gardens and what was once the village pump. This is a great spot for an early picnic. Now walk back in the direction from where you came and take the first right up **Pinfold Road**, past the shop and the old-fashioned fuel pumps. Continue up the hill and turn left at the T-junction past the **Fox and Hounds Inn** and **Castle Inn**. **St James' church** is also to your right. The road curves to the right past lovely rows of cottages and joins **Station Road**.

Continue away from the village centre, looking left for good views over the castle mound. Cross the disused railway line, pass the quarries to your right, walk straight over the crossroads and continue out of the village. The landscape here is beautiful rolling farmland but stay on the quiet road, as the grass verges are specially protected to maintain its wildlife. Pass two wooded areas and you can soon see a spring leading to a pond in the valley to your left through the trees. Shortly after passing a farm track leading right, take the footpath left heading down a track. Enjoy the pretty lake to your right surrounded by rolling hills.

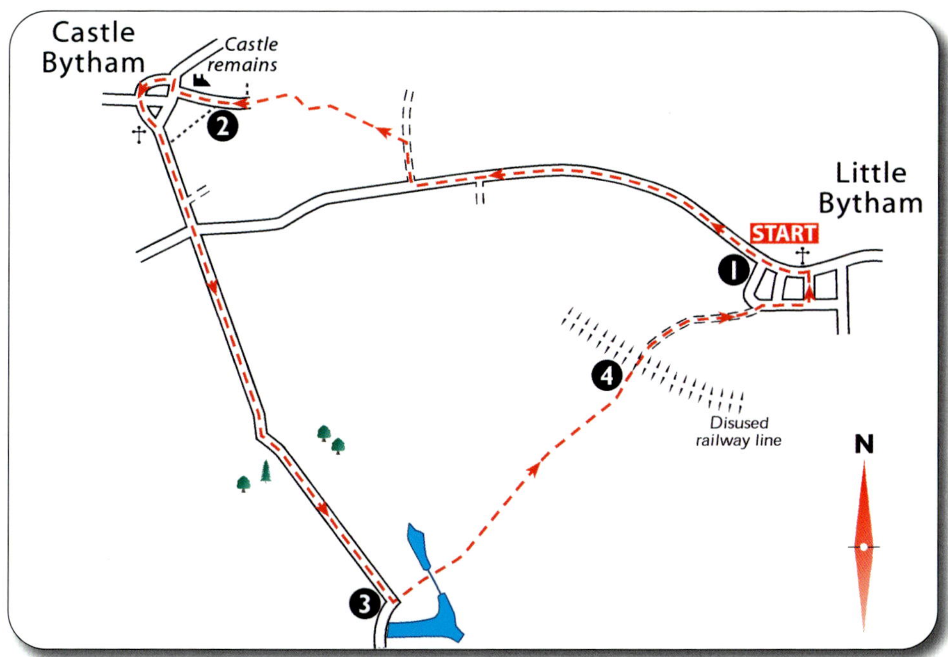

■ *The castle mound is still clearly visible on the hillside* ■

3 The track leads past beautiful cottages on your right and over a stream. Once in the field take the track leading slightly away from the fence and up the hill with the rabbit burrows to your left. Continue uphill with the wooded area on your right. At the top walk through the gate, across the track and through the next gate straight ahead. Follow the hedge running parallel to your right and, when you reach the tennis courts, walk between two narrow hedges until you reach a field. Continue straight on with the hedge on your right. After crossing a stile, take a quick left then right, where there is a good view over the surrounding landscape. Follow the hedge on your left as the field becomes narrower. At the end continue along the same track, following a hedge to your right. When the hedge ends, follow the track left before taking a sharp right after a few paces down a slope in almost the opposite direction from where you were walking before. This leads down into a gulley under the disused railway line.

4 Follow the tall hedge leading gradually right, walk through the gate and continue straight ahead along a track with a stream to your left and a pond behind it among the trees. Ignore the footbridge to your left and continue over the stile, past an old mill, and take the small path that forks left from the main tack. This leads to the village. Take the footbridge over the beck, with the ford to the right, and walk along a lovely lane teeming with delightful old cottages and with the church straight ahead. When you reach the T-junction, turn left and the road leads back to the start.

17 Carlton Scroop to Ancaster

FOOTPATHS FOR FITNESS

In the Steps of the Romans

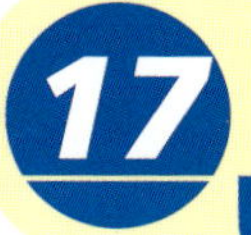

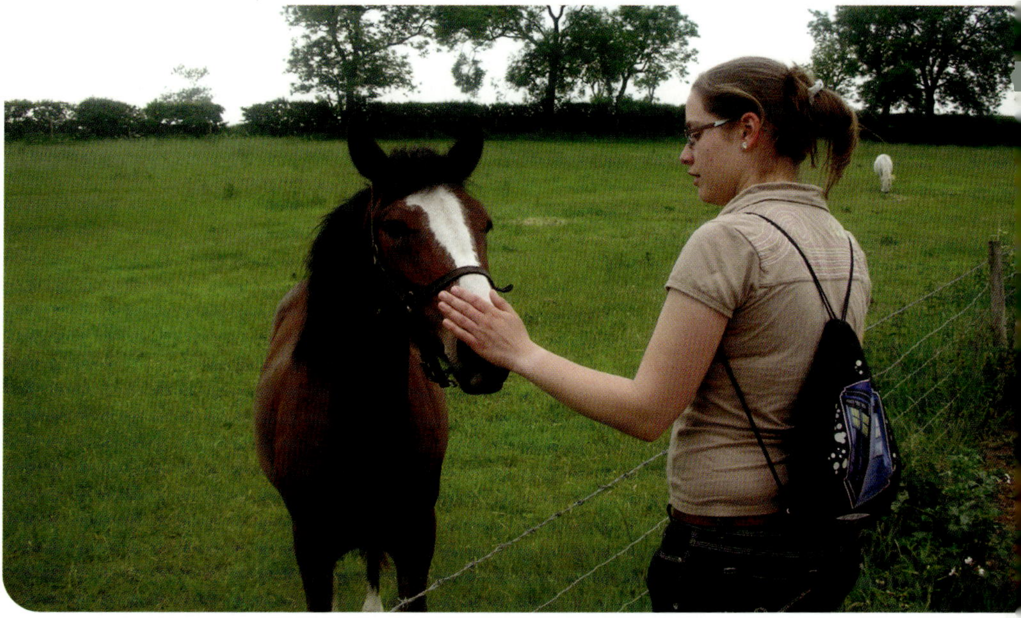

■ *A chance to meet the locals* ■

This walk is a good test of your endurance, particularly in the second half, because there are few places to stop and rest. But you will be rewarded with delightful views from one of the few elevated spots in the region. You can also enjoy the beautiful village of **Ancaster**, which has been of such historical significance that Channel 4's *Time Team* conducted an excavation here. The village was the site of an old Roman settlement and grass banks still mark where parts of the old wall would have been. Many Roman coins have been found here, as well as skeletons from the time and carvings of Roman gods and goddesses. Look for buildings in the region made from Ancaster stone, which has been used to build many great buildings including Belvoir Castle and Wollaton Hall.

Continue along **Sudbrook Road** and see if you can spot a white peacock in a garden to your right. You soon leave the village and are walking along the foot of a hill to your left. The road cuts through the wide valley and when it straightens you can see the railway line running parallel to the right. Ignore the first two footpaths to the right and take the next one after the grey house on your right. Keep your eyes peeled because the sign is tricky to spot. Cross the field diagonally left, aiming for the modern red-brick house. Cross the stile over the wooden fence in front and follow the small street ahead, before continuing through a small gap between a wall and a fence at the end. A driveway takes you to the road and you're now in the heart of **Sudbrook**. This small, quiet village is adorned with pretty grey-brick houses. Turn right and follow the road when it curves round to the left. At the junction follow it to the right and take the farm track left just after the level crossing.

2 The track takes you through the middle of two arable fields, gradually leading you further away from the railway line to the left. When you reach the footpath signposts take the path right. You soon pass the entrance to **Moor Closes** on the right, an area of boggy grassland under conservation. A short walk takes you around the site if you feel tempted but prepare to get your feet wet if you do. Continue along the dirt track with trees either side and walk straight on at the footpath signpost. Soon you'll see a stone wall to your left and a huge field to the right. There are two benches available when you reach the cemetery on your right. Soon after the cemetery turn left through the gate into the churchyard, where there are more benches should you want to stop for a picnic.

GRADE: 2
ESTIMATED CALORIE BURN: 590

Distance: 6 miles
Time: 3 hours
Terrain: Mostly along dirt paths and tracks. The route climbs and descends one small hill.
Number of stiles: 1
Starting point: Carlton Scroop. GR 953453.
How to get there: From Grantham head north along the A607. When you reach Carlton Scroop, take the second right on the corner into Sudbrook Road and park on the verge. Buses run to Carlton Scroop every 30 minutes from Grantham and Lincoln.
OS map: Landranger 130 Grantham, Sleaford & Bourne.
Refreshments: Ancaster has a pub, the Ermine Way (tel. 01400 230697) and a convenience store.

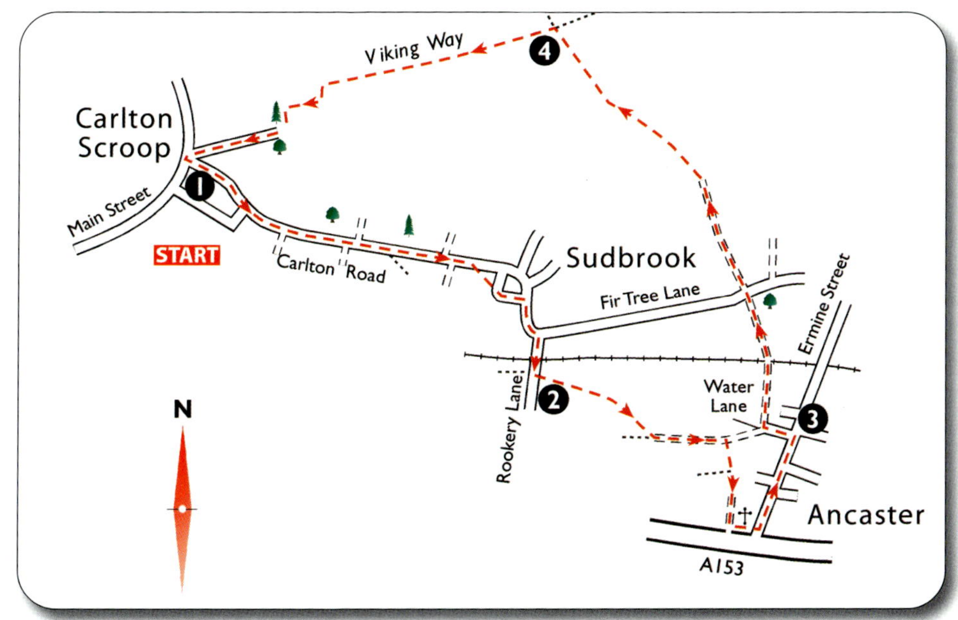

Walk through here until you reach **Ermine Street**. This is part of the Roman road linking London to the north. It is now **Ancaster**'s main street and has rows of beautiful old buildings made from Ancaster stone either side of it. Turn left so you pass first the church to your left, then a convenience store, a pub and a butcher's shop. You pass a cricket field to your right where there are more benches if you fancy having your picnic here.

3 Turn left down **Water Lane**, opposite the post office, then when you reach a footpath junction turn right along a paved track slightly uphill. This section is mostly uphill but is a very gradual slope and shouldn't be too strenuous. Continue across the level crossing passing Ancaster train station on your right and follow the lane up the gentle hill. Cross over the road and a dirt track leads you straight on between farm fields. Here you reach a ridge where on a clear day there are great views west over **Sudbrook** and beyond, and back where you came from over **Ancaster**. The track continues for a while, veering left and through a gap in the hedge. When you reach the second hedge, don't turn right but walk through the gap and continue. Eventually it joins a wider track which you follow round to the right for around 400 yards. When you reach the T-junction there is a concrete slab you can sit on should you need a break. Turn left at the junction, joining the **Viking Way**, so that the BT tower is in the direction of 11 o'clock.

4 Now you can gather pace for the final big push of this walk. Follow the track straight for around ¾ mile, where you will notice a crumbling brick wall, then a hedge running parallel to you on your right. Follow the hedge when it swings to the left then back round to the right again. Now you start the descent, turning left again with the trees to the right. The track bends back round to the right and straight down the hill, passing the BT tower to the left. The track becomes paved and leads you all the way to the road. Once there, turn left to where your car will be waiting for you at the side of the road.

■ *St Martin's church* ■

18 Freiston Shore to the Pilgrims' Memorial

FOOTPATHS FOR FITNESS

A Walk in the Wilderness

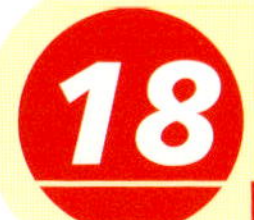

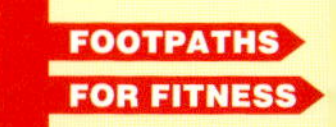

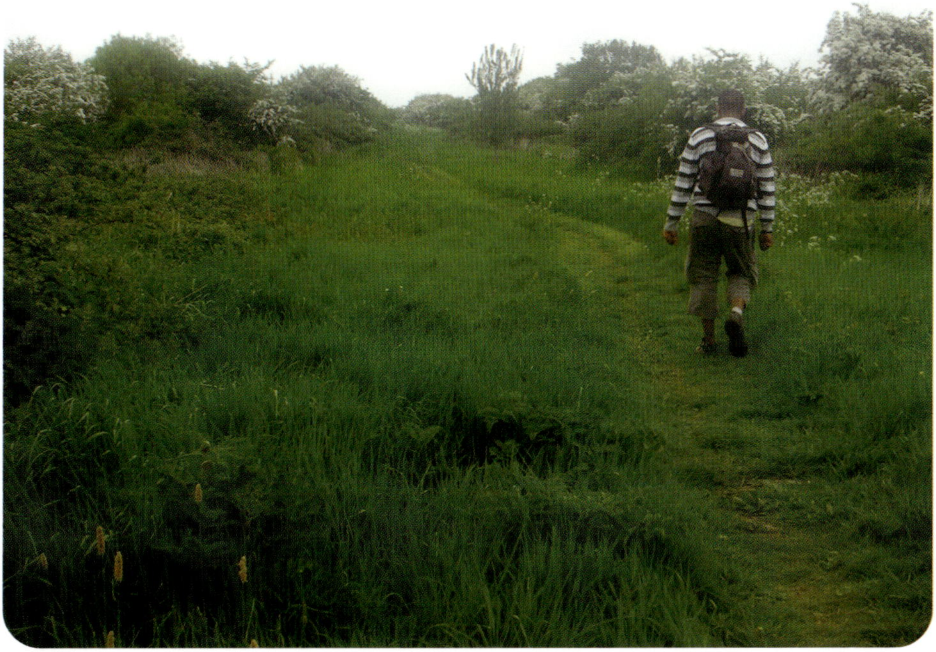

■ *A world away from the marshes* ■

Welcome to the Lincolnshire wilderness. Much of the county's coastline is uninhabited, with marshland extending into the distance. It often resembles an early scene from *Great Expectations* and can be mysterious and beautiful in its own way. The walk captures the essence of this wild coastline. The weather can be blustery to say the least, but being situated in The Wash, the ground is flat so you can always keep up a good pace. The rewards are fantastic too. The walk begins at Freiston Shore – a reclaimed section of salt marsh and a lagoon that is a haven for birdlife. You will see the memorial built for the Pilgrim Fathers, who bravely set sail for new lands across the Atlantic. And you have the unique experience of walking straight through the middle of a prison!

GRADE: 3
ESTIMATED CALORIE BURN: 700

Distance: 8 miles
Time: 4 hours
Terrain: Flat with mostly grassy paths, roads and tracks.
Number of stiles: 9
Starting point: The car park at Freiston Shore Nature Reserve. GR 397424.
How to get there: From the A52 east of Boston, turn right at Haltoft End towards Freiston. Take the second left in Freiston village then continue east towards Freiston Shore Nature Reserve, where there is a car park.
OS map: Landranger 131 Boston & Spalding.
Refreshments: It is worth packing a picnic as there are no shops or pubs along the route.

1 The best way to get a flavour for the area is to start by walking the triangular circuit of the lagoon. As you face the lagoon from the car park, turn right to loop anti-clockwise. After 250 yards there is a hide to your left, giving close-up views of the many waders, gulls and geese scurrying around looking for food while making a terrific noise. The path eventually leads to a gate, which you walk through and head up the bank. Here you're greeted by the orange, brown and black colours of the salt marshes leading to the distant sea. Turn left, then left again and, as you walk, you'll see where the banks to your right have been purposefully breached to allow the tide to come in and enable the nature reserve to thrive. To your left is an elevated view of the lagoon and there are several benches along the way looking over it. Keep walking along the grassy footpath until you reach a gate. Here, turn left and walk back towards the car park. Stay on the bank so you pass the car park on your left, cross the entrance and continue along the footpath directly opposite. Six gates then lead you rather uncomfortably through the gardens of those who live in the neighbouring hamlet here.

2 Continue along the top of the bank past the many old pillboxes that can provide good shelter if it rains. The wetlands continue to your left, with the sea bank behind and, after around 500 yards, a bench overlooks another lagoon if you fancy a little more bird watching. If not, follow the path along the grass bank until you eventually reach **North Sea Camp**, an open prison where the politician and writer Jeffrey Archer once 'stayed'. Remarkably, the footpath runs straight through the grounds. Make sure you don't stray even to the sides of the bank because the security staff on site are very strict. Don't continue along the bank when it follows a road round to the right. Instead, cross the road and continue straight on (following the sign that says Maintenance Department) and after crossing two stiles you will leave the prison grounds. Continue for another 400 yards as the bank curves to the right. Cross the stile straight on, ignoring the one to the left, down the side of the bank and walk straight on. Follow the grass until it ends and then continue along the footpath across the field. This can be muddy and the path can be unclear, so aim slightly to the right of the house ahead.

3 When you reach the road, turn left towards the bank. When you reach it and the car park is on your left, climb over the stile and you're now on the north bank of **The Haven**. Over the other side of the water is **The Scalp** – miles of bleak marshland with not a house in sight. Turn right and continue along the bank, which at first runs right next to the water before zigzagging its way to a dam. Cross the dam over the bridge and along a dirt road. You will notice the scenery momentarily changes from marshland wilderness to a country lane with small paddocks and hedgerows. Follow the track for around 150 yards. Just before reaching a driveway, with stone pillars either

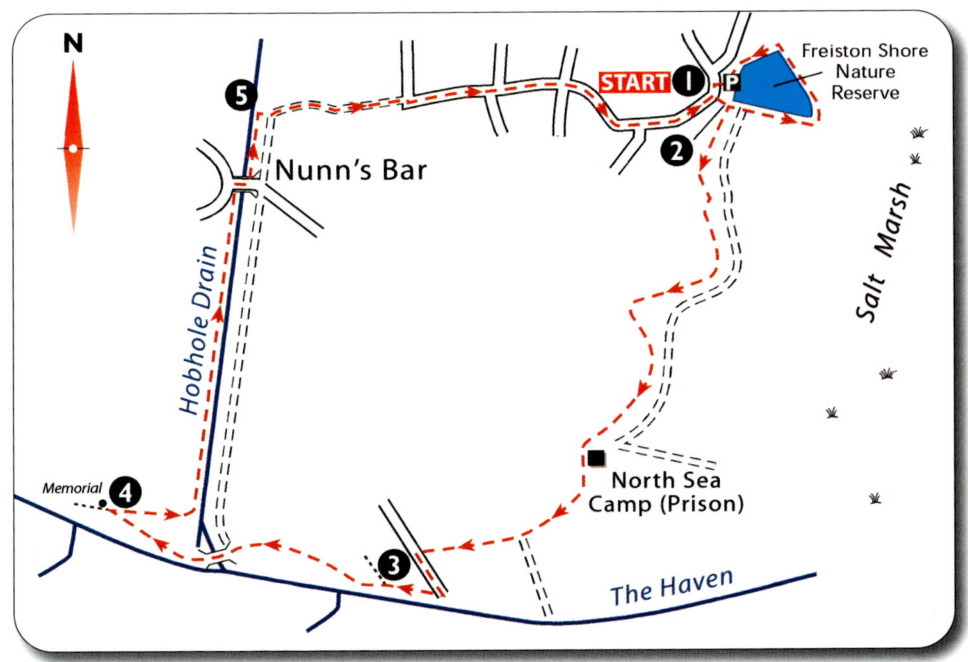

side leading to the house ahead, take the path left that goes over a stile back to the estuary. Turn right and when the bank turns to the left, climb the stile and continue straight on, through a field with a small pond either side and then up the bank to the memorial.

This modest granite monument was built in 1957 to commemorate the Pilgrim Fathers' first attempt to flee to the new land, later known as the United States of America, in the 17th century amid problems of betrayal, bad weather, disease and bureaucracy. Nearby is a car park with an information board. The field next to the monument is a good place for a picnic because there are benches and it's in a hollow, which means you are sheltered from the wind.

■ *The memorial to the Pilgrim Fathers* ■

4 Walk back through the gate and stay left along the top of the bank furthest from the estuary. Continue through a small gate then, after a stile, down a narrow path between two hedges, down some steps and turn left when you reach the river, the **Hobhole Drain**. The path continues parallel to the river on your right and is picturesquely set between hedgerows and trees. After 1,500 yards along the river bank you reach the tiny hamlet of **Nun's Bar**. Turn right, crossing the bridge, before taking an immediate turn left to walk parallel to the river, now on your left.

5 After 200 yards a track running alongside the footpath heads right. Follow this for 900 yards until you reach the corner of a lane. Continue straight on until you reach a road junction. Turn left here then immediately right, following the sign to **Freiston Shore**. Ignore any turnings left and right and continue through scattered cottages until you reach the entrance to **Freiston Shore Nature Reserve** on your right.

19 Thurlby, Witham-on-the-Hill and Manthorpe

On the Trail of the Giant Oak

FOOTPATHS FOR FITNESS

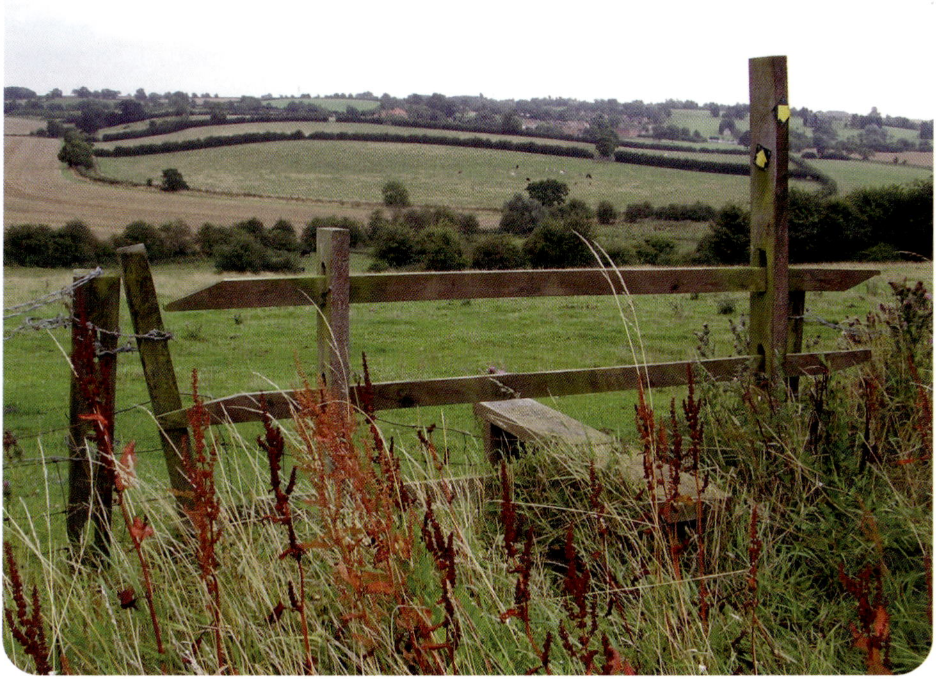

■ *Looking east to Toft* ■

This walk takes you back to the beautiful rolling landscape south of Grantham and west of Bourne. It involves strolling along the winding **River Glen**, admiring the grand houses in **Witham-on-the-Hill** and even taking a look at a record-breaking tree. The **giant oak** at **Bowthorpe Park Farm**, near **Manthorpe**, made its name in the *Guinness Book of Records* for being the 'fattest' tree in Britain. It is believed to be over 1,000 years old, has a 40 ft circumference, and a former tenant at the farm once squeezed 39 people into its hollow centre! As a walk, it is far from flat, but there are no hills to worry you, especially if you have already walked from Tealby to Walesby. It is long, but if you give yourself several hours and the weather is kind it will be a very pleasant experience.

1 Walk up **Wood Lane** and after just a few paces take the footpath left along a gravel drive. Keep to the right, next to the hedge, when you continue through the garden. At the end, cross the stile to go straight across a paddock, then go over another stile and across a footbridge which will take you to a large field. Turn diagonally right, aiming just to the right of the electricity pylon situated at a 2 o'clock angle. Cross the wooden bridge at the end, being careful not to trip over the ankle-height wooden planks crossing the path. Continue straight across the next field towards the trees, taking a left turn when you reach the track. After a few yards a footpath takes you right. Aim for the far left-hand corner of the field situated left of the hedge. This takes you to a wooden bridge, after which turn left along the path leading straight up the hill – make sure you take the path leading gradually away from the left-hand side of the field. The top is a good place to look back over **Bourne** (at 4 o'clock), the **Fens** stretching miles into the distance and the wind farm. Cross the bridge and go over the stile before keeping left through the next two fields.

2 Cross the main road and take the tiny lane down the slope straight ahead. It leads to a crossroads in the tiny hamlet of **Lound**. Walk straight on at the crossroads and continue as the windy road becomes a dirt track after the final delightful cottage. The track continues and you find yourself surrounded by small hills on all sides. Cross the river and enjoy the sight of the gentle valley straight ahead. The path first veers left, then right. Follow

GRADE: 3
ESTIMATED CALORIE BURN: 740

Distance: 8 miles
Time: 4 hours
Terrain: There are several small hills, with a range of terrain that can be muddy in places after wet weather.
Number of stiles: 14
Starting point: Wood Lane, Thurlby. GR 093174.
How to get there: From Bourne take the A15 south. When you reach Thurlby, turn right along Northorpe Lane and park just before Wood Lane. Buses run to Thurlby every 30 minutes from Bourne and Peterborough.
OS map: Landranger 130 Grantham, Sleaford & Bourne.
Refreshments: The Six Bells pub passed at point 3 of the walk serves food (tel. 01778 590360).

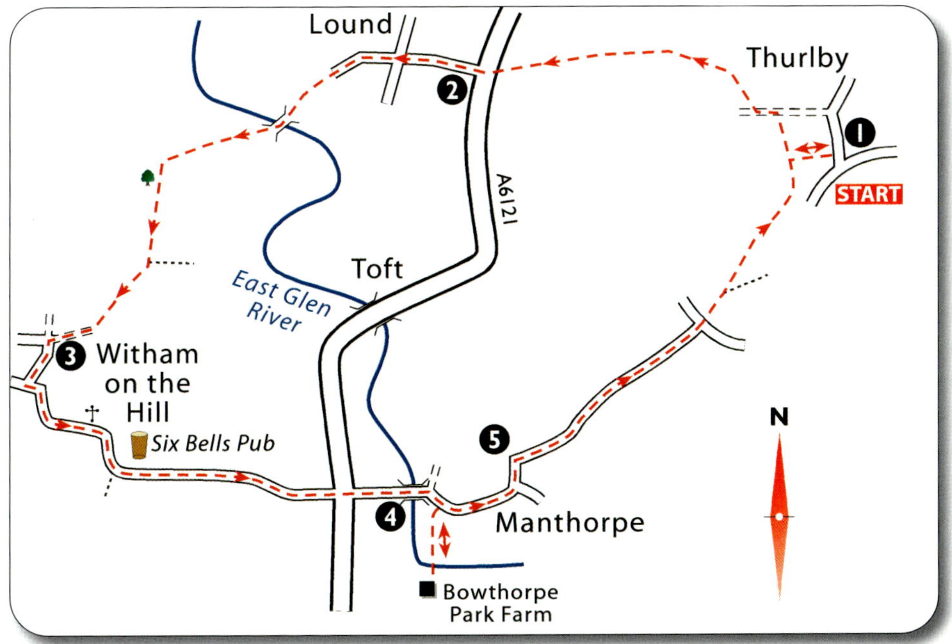

the hedge to the right of the field – see the golf course in the distance on your left. Where the field curves left, continue straight on up the small path leading into a small wood. At the footpath junction, take a left turn and keep to the left of the wood. Take the stile heading out of the wood and enjoy the sight to your left of the **East Glen river** with the village of **Toft** behind. Walk slightly uphill to the end of the hedge ahead. Cross the stile here and stay to the left of the field. When the hedge stops continue straight through the field. The path isn't always clear here, but aim for the two tallest trees straight ahead and turn right when you reach a track near the end of the giant field.

3 The track heads downhill and becomes a lane. Follow the lane round to the left between the houses, cross the beck and continue up the other side of the hill to the main road. You are now in **Witham-on-the-Hill** and when you turn left at the T-junction you can see the stocks on your left that were used in medieval times to punish petty criminals. You soon pass a bench to your left looking out over the park and to the church beyond, which could make a good picnic spot. The street takes you past an old hall which is now a prep school, past the peculiarly shaped church, between the beautiful grey stone buildings and past the **Six Bells pub**, which serves hot food should you need a bite to eat. Continue along the road, where there is a pavement all the way, as well as several benches. Cross the main road and continue straight into **Manthorpe.**

4 When you enter the village, follow the road round to the right and on the next corner take the footpath to the stile on your right. If you are feeling too tired to take the deviation

■ *The forge in Manthorpe* ■

to the giant oak then continue along the road. Otherwise cross the stile and follow the fence straight on and round to the left. Fork away from the fence a little and aim for the stile in the fence in front of you. Walk straight across the field, cross a small footbridge and over a stile to go up the hill to the footpath signs in front of the barns. Once in the farmyard turn left, then quickly right up to the gate and enjoy a great view of the fattest tree in Britain! If you're really keen, you can go inside it for a charge of £2.50 and kids get to visit for free. Once you've had a good look, head back to the village – down the hill, over the stream and stile, across the fields via another stile and right to a further stile. Turn right to follow the road, with largely older houses on the right and newer ones on the left.

5 Continue left, past the beautiful old village forge and out of **Manthorpe** village, keeping to the road and heading up the gradual hill. When you reach the road junction take the footpath straight ahead between the fence and the hedge. Over the brow of the hill you're greeted to a great view of the **Fens** once more. Climb the stile and take the footpath forking left, cutting through the field with the wind farm at 1 o'clock. You can gather pace as you head downhill, following the hedge on the right for the second half of the giant field. Turn left at the end of the field then a quick right over the bridge, and retrace your steps from the start through the paddock, the garden, down the drive and to the finish.

20 Goulceby to Belchford

Stunning Views Abound

■ *Above Belchford* ■

This walk, set in the heart of the Lincolnshire Wolds, is a wonderfully enjoyable way to finish your series of fitness treks through the county. Starting in the tiny peaceful lanes of spacious **Goulceby** village, it takes you along a stream to **Scamblesby**, then over the hill to pretty **Belchford** before returning over the hills again. It provides excellent views across the valleys, and the fact that a big cat was spotted near here recently only adds to the interest!

1 From the car parking space, turn left up **Shop Lane** and at the end cross the stile ahead and walk to the right of the grass field, noting the large house to your left and the pond to the right. The path takes you over a stile through a small copse and along a boardwalk. Ignore the right turn, cross the track and continue with the stream on your right. Stay with the stream through the gentle valley crossing a stile along the path to reach **Asterby**

GRADE: 3
ESTIMATED CALORIE BURN: 780

Distance: 8½ miles
Time: 4 hours
Terrain: Mostly dirt paths, can be muddy in places after rain, much of the walk is up and down rolling landscape.
Number of stiles: 6
Starting point: Shop Lane, Goulceby. GR 255794.
How to get there: From the B1225 north from Horncastle turn right, taking you into Goulceby along Top Lane. Once in the village take the second right, Butt Lane, and park on the left before the left turn into Shop Lane, where there is space for cars.
OS map: Landranger 122 Skegness & Horncastle.
Refreshments: The Green Man pub at Scamblesby (tel. 01507 343282) and the Bluebell at Belchford (tel. 01507 533602) both serve food.

Lane. Take a quick right-left (crossing the stream) and continue along the footpath with the stream now to your left. Continue straight on when you reach a small lake to the right and after you pass a wooded area to your left you need to cross the stream again at the signpost. Continue with the stream once again on your right, enjoying the open landscape with hills to your left, right and straight ahead.

Follow the stream as it cuts left, then right through a wood and over a small bridge. With the stream still on your right you'll pass a reed pond to the left before reaching the main road. Follow the path straight over the other side, cross the wooden bridge and walk to the next road. You're now in the centre of **Scamblesby** and to your left is the **Green Man pub** if you need a break. Otherwise turn right and take the first street left, South Street, passing the village hall to your right.

2 Continue up the slight hill and eventually turn right up **Mill Lane**. The scattered houses along this stretch seem to continue forever. Once you reach the dead end, dog-leg around the hedge on the right so you continue up a mud track with the hedge to your left. The hills are now close ahead with woodland at the top. When you get the choice of two tracks take the one forking right and when you reach the gate the real climb begins. Aim for the far right corner of the grass field then, after the double gate, walk straight uphill with the wood on your right. At the top is a great view back over the valley, and a plastic black cat stares at you from inside the hedge.

Walk through the gate and continue down to the left of the hedge with the conservation area and various pools of water to your right. After undulating, the path dips between two hedges before angling left down the hill. Turn left at the end of the field with the hedge on your right, and after 20 yards take the bridge over the stream. Turn immediately left and follow the field around to the right. Keep to the left of all fields until you come to the road. You have reached **Belchford**, home of the annual downhill home-made soap-box event. It is also the village where in 1536 the vicar of the time was hanged, drawn and quartered for leading a rebellion against the Crown, during the reformation of the English Church.

3 The **Bluebell pub** is to your left should you need to refresh yourself. This walk instead takes you right along the road for around 400 yards. Just after a right bend and before the road starts uphill there is a hard-to-spot footpath right between two houses. This soon joins a bigger track and goes gradually uphill until you reach a group of holiday cottages. A bench here looks

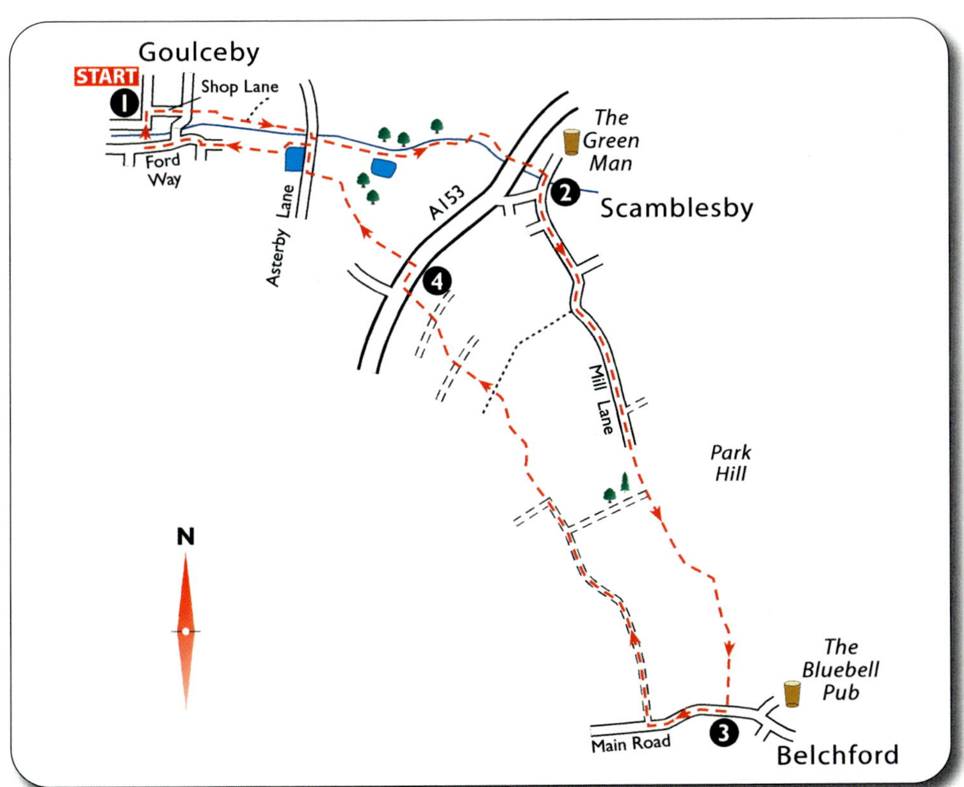

south-west over the conservation area of pools and through the valleys into the distance. This is a prime picnic spot and the views are stunning. Continue straight on over a paved area and up to a gate at the top of the hill, ignoring the drive as it turns to the left – this is the last significant climb of the walk. The spot gives you views over the valleys both sides of the hill.

■ *Stepping up a gear on the way back to Goulceby* ■

Keep to the left next to the hedge and walk along the ridge. Continue in the same direction through the next field and when you start to descend aim to the right of the small trees at the end of the field. The bridleway is clearly marked downhill, cutting straight through several fields. You then reach a boggy section, following a line of trees with a small pond to your left. After a second pond the track leads to the road.

4 Turn right and take the footpath left just before the **Scamblesby** sign. Continue through a gate and aim just to the left of a conifer wood. When you reach the trees cross a bridge in the small dip. The path undulates with the wood on your right. Continue until you reach the road, **Asterby Lane**, with the reservoir behind. Turn right and after 50 yards take a left just before the road bridge. Take the steps up the bank of the reservoir, turn right with the water to your left and follow the bank round to the left before taking the steps down to the double stile on your right. Continue with the hedge on your right and after the final stile take a quick left-right and stay to the left of the field. Ignore the green path sign over the stile straight ahead and instead take a quick right-left and continue next to the horse paddock with the wooden fence to your right. Walk straight through the yard and through a small gap to **Goulceby Lane**. When it joins **Ford Way** continue straight ahead. After 200 yards, shortly after the phone box and before the T-junction, take the footpath right between two hedges. Cross the bridge and continue straight up the street back to your car.